PRACTICE - ASSESS - DIAGNOSE

180 Days of SCIENCE
for Third Grade

W9-BDC-515

Author
Melissa Iwinski

SHELL EDUCATION

Earth & Space
Life
Physical

Publishing Credits

Corinne Burton, M.A.Ed., *Publisher*
Conni Medina, M.A.Ed., *Managing Editor*
Emily R. Smith, M.A.Ed., *Content Director*
Shaun Bernadou, *Art Director*
Lynette Ordoñez, *Editor*

Image Credits

All images from iStock and/or Shutterstock.

Standards

© 2014 Mid-continent Research for Education and Learning (McREL)
NGSS Lead States. 2013. Next Generation Science Standards: For States, By States.
Washington, DC: The National Academies Press.

For information on how this resource meets national and other state standards, see pages 10–13. You may also review this information by visiting our website at www.teachercreatedmaterials.com/administrators/correlations/ and following the on-screen directions.

Shell Education

A division of Teacher Created Materials
5301 Oceanus Drive
Huntington Beach, CA 92649-1030
www.tcmpub.com/shell-education

ISBN 978-1-4258-1409-0
©2018 Shell Educational Publishing, Inc.

Table of Contents

Introduction

With today's science and technology, there are more resources than ever to help students understand how the world works. Information about science experiments you can do at home is widely available online. Many students have experience with physics concepts from games.

While students may be familiar with many of the topics discussed in this book, it is not uncommon for them to have misconceptions about certain subjects. It is important for students to learn how to apply scientific practices in a classroom setting and within their lives.

Science is the study of the physical and natural world through observation and experiment. Not only is it important for students to learn scientific facts, but it is important for them to develop a thirst for knowledge. This leads to students who are anxious to learn and who understand how to follow practices that will lead them to the answers they seek.

The Need for Practice

To be successful in science, students must understand how people interact with the physical world. They must not only master scientific practices but also learn how to look at the world with curiosity. Through repeated practice, students will learn how a variety of factors affect the world in which they live.

Understanding Assessment

In addition to providing opportunities for frequent practice, teachers must be able to assess students' scientific understandings. This allows teachers to adequately address students' misconceptions, build on their current understandings, and challenge them appropriately. Assessment is a long-term process that involves careful analysis of student responses from discussions, projects, or practice sheets. The data gathered from assessments should be used to inform instruction: slow down, speed up, or reteach. This type of assessment is called *formative assessment*.

How to Use This Book

Weekly Structure

All 36 weeks of this book follow a regular weekly structure. The book is divided into three sections: Life Science, Physical Science, and Earth and Space Science. The book is structured to give students a strong foundation on which to build throughout the year. It is also designed to adequately prepare them for state standardized tests.

Each week focuses on one topic. Day 1 sets the stage by providing background information on the topic that students will need throughout the week. In Day 2, students analyze data related to the topic. Day 3 leads students through developing scientific questions. Day 4 guides students through planning a solution. Finally, Day 5 helps students communicate results from observations or investigations.

 Day 1—Learning Content: Students will read grade-appropriate content and answer questions about it.

 Day 2—Analyzing Data: Students will analyze scientific data and answer questions about it.

 Day 3—Developing Questions: Students will read a scenario related to the topic, answer questions, and formulate a scientific question about the information.

 Day 4—Planning Solutions: Students will read a scenario related to the topic, answer questions, and develop a solution or plan an investigation.

 Day 5—Communicating Results: Students accurately communicate the results of an investigation or demonstrate what they learned throughout the week.

Three Strands of Science

This book allows students to explore the three strands of science: life science, physical science, and earth and space science. Life science teaches students about the amazing living things on our planet and how they interact in ecosystems. Physical science introduces students to physics and chemistry concepts that will lay the groundwork for deeper understanding later in their education. Earth and space science familiarizes students with the wonders of the cosmos and the relationships between the sun, Earth, moon, and stars.

How to Use This Book (cont.)

Weekly Topics

The following chart shows the weekly focus topics that are covered during each week of instruction.

Unit	Week	Science Topic
Life Science	1	Why Animals Live in Groups
	2	Animal Jobs within Groups
	3	Life Cycle of Plants
	4	Life Cycle of Animals
	5	How Fossils Form
	6	Studying Fossils
	7	Desert Plants and Animals
	8	Habitats
	9	Parents and Offspring
	10	How Living Things Affect Each Other
	11	Variations in Animals
	12	Changes to Environments
Physical Science	1	Pulling
	2	Rolling Balls
	3	Pushing
	4	Seesaws
	5	Swinging
	6	Spinning
	7	Creating Static Electricity
	8	Magnets
	9	Effects of Static Electricity
	10	Super Magnets
	11	Keeping Things Closed with Magnets
	12	Using Magnets for Clean-Up
Earth and Space Science	1	Winter
	2	Spring
	3	Summer
	4	Fall
	5	Deserts
	6	Rainforests
	7	Tundras
	8	Temperate Climates
	9	Flooding
	10	Melting Snow and Ice with Salt
	11	Wind
	12	Sun Damage

How to Use This Book *(cont.)*

Best Practices for This Series

- Use the practice pages to introduce important science topics to your students.

- Use the Weekly Topics chart on page 5 to align the content to what you're covering in class. Then, treat the pages in this book as jumping off points for that content.

- Use the practice pages as formative assessment of the science strands and key topics.

- Use the weekly themes to engage students in content that is new to them.

- Encourage students to independently learn more about the topics introduced in this series.

- Lead teacher-directed discussions of the vocabulary and concepts presented in some of the more complex weeks.

- Support students in practicing the varied types of questions asked throughout the practice pages.

- When possible, have students participate in hands-on activities to answer the questions they generate and do the investigations they plan.

Using the Resources

An answer key for all days can be found on pages 194–205. Rubrics for Day 3 (developing questions), Day 4 (planning solutions), and Day 5 (communicating results) can be found on pages 210–212 and in the Digital Resources. Use the answer keys and rubrics to assess students' work. Be sure to share these rubrics with students so that they know what is expected of them.

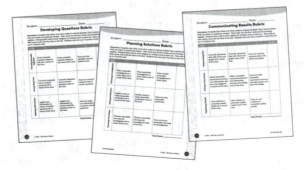

How to Use This Book *(cont.)*

Diagnostic Assessment

Teachers can use the practice pages as diagnostic assessments. The data analysis tools included with the book enable teachers or parents to quickly score students' work and monitor their progress. Teachers and parents can see which skills students may need to target further to develop proficiency.

Students will learn science content, how to analyze data, how to develop scientific questions, how to plan solutions, and how to accurately communicate results. You can assess students' learning using the answer key for all days. Rubrics are also provided on pages 210–212 for Days 3–5 to help you further assess key analytical skills that are needed for success with the scientific practices. Then, record their scores on the Practice Page Item Analysis sheets (pages 213–215). These charts are provided as PDFs, Microsoft Word® files, and Microsoft Excel® files. Teachers can input data into the electronic files directly, or they can print the pages.

To Complete the Practice Page Analysis Charts

- Write or type students' names in the far-left column. Depending on the number of students, more than one copy of the form may be needed or you may need to add rows.

  - The science strands are indicated across the tops of the charts.

  - Students should be assessed every four weeks, as indicated in the first rows of the charts.

- For each student, evaluate his or her work over the past four weeks using the answer key for Days 1 and 2 and the rubrics for Days 3–5.

- Review students' work for the weeks indicated in the chart. For example, if using the *Life Science Analysis Chart* for the first time, review students' work from weeks 1–4. Add the scores for Days 1 and 2 for each student, and record those in the appropriate columns. Then, write students' rubric scores for Days 3–5 in the corresponding columns. Use these scores as benchmarks to determine how each student is performing.

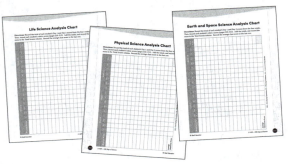

Digital Resources

The Digital Resources contain digital copies of the rubrics, analysis sheets, and standards correlations. See page 216 for more information.

How to Use This Book *(cont.)*

Using the Results to Differentiate Instruction

Once results are gathered and analyzed, teachers can use the results to inform the way they differentiate instruction. The data can help determine which science skills and topics are the most difficult for students and which students need additional instructional support and continued practice.

Whole-Class Support

The results of the diagnostic analysis may show that the entire class is struggling with certain science topics. If these concepts have been taught in the past, this indicates that further instruction or reteaching is necessary. If these concepts have not been taught in the past, this data is a great preassessment and may demonstrate that students do not have a working knowledge of the concepts. Thus, careful planning for the length of the unit(s) or lesson(s) must be considered, and additional front-loading may be required.

Small-Group or Individual Support

The results of the diagnostic analysis may show that an individual student or a small group of students is struggling with certain science skills. If these concepts have been taught in the past, this indicates that further instruction or reteaching is necessary. Consider pulling these students aside to instruct them further on the concepts while others are working independently. Students may also benefit from extra practice using games or computer-based resources.

Teachers can also use the results to help identify proficient individual students or groups of students who are ready for enrichment or above-grade-level instruction. These students may benefit from independent learning contracts or more challenging activities.

Standards Correlations

Shell Education is committed to producing educational materials that are research and standards based. In this effort, we have correlated all of our products to the academic standards of all 50 states, the District of Columbia, the Department of Defense Dependents Schools, and all Canadian provinces.

How to Find Standards Correlations

To print a customized correlation report of this product for your state, visit our website at **www.teachercreatedmaterials.com/administrators/correlations/** and follow the on-screen directions. If you require assistance in printing correlation reports, please contact our Customer Service Department at 1-877-777-3450.

Purpose and Intent of Standards

The Every Student Succeeds Act (ESSA) mandates that all states adopt challenging academic standards that help students meet the goal of college and career readiness. While many states already adopted academic standards prior to ESSA, the act continues to hold states accountable for detailed and comprehensive standards.

Standards are designed to focus instruction and guide adoption of curricula. Standards are statements that describe the criteria necessary for students to meet specific academic goals. They define the knowledge, skills, and content students should acquire at each level. Standards are also used to develop standardized tests to evaluate students' academic progress. Teachers are required to demonstrate how their lessons meet state standards. State standards are used in the development of all of our products, so educators can be assured they meet the academic requirements of each state.

McREL Compendium

Each year, McREL analyzes state standards and revises the compendium to produce a general compilation of national standards. The standards listed on page 10 support the objectives presented throughout the weeks.

Next Generation Science Standards

This set of national standards aims to incorporate knowledge and process standards into a cohesive framework. The standards listed on pages 10–13 support the objectives presented throughout the weeks.

Standards Correlations *(cont.)*

180 Days of Science is designed to give students daily practice in the three strands of science. The weeks support the McREL standards and NGSS performance expectations listed in the charts below.

McREL Standards		
Standard	**Weeks**	**Unit**
Knows that an organism's patterns of behavior are related to the nature of that organism's environment.	1, 2	Life Science
Knows that plants and animals progress through life cycles of birth, growth and development, reproduction, and death; the details of these life cycles are different for different organisms.	3, 4	Life Science
Knows that fossils can be compared to one another and to living organisms to observe their similarities and differences.	5, 6	Life Science
Knows that changes in the environment can have different effects on different organisms.	7, 8, 12	Life Science
Knows that many characteristics of plants and animals are inherited from its parents, and other characteristics result from an individual's interactions with the environment.	9–11	Life Science
Knows that when force is applied to an object, the object either speeds up, slows down, or goes in a different direction.	1–3	Physical Science
Knows the relationship between the strength of a force and its effect on an object.	1–3	Physical Science
Knows that an object's motion can be described by tracing and measuring its position over time.	3–6	Physical Science
Knows that electrically charged material pulls on all other materials and can attract or repel other charged materials.	7, 9	Physical Science
Knows that magnets attract and repel each other and attract certain kinds of other materials.	8, 10–12	Physical Science

Next Generation Science Standards					
Unit	**Week**	**Performance Expectation**	**Science and Engineering Practices**	**Disciplinary Core Ideas**	**Cross-Cutting Concepts**
Life Science	1	Construct an argument that some animals form groups that help members survive.	Engaging in Argument from Evidence	Social Interactions and Group Behavior	Systems and System Models
	2	Construct an argument that some animals form groups that help members survive.	Engaging in Argument from Evidence	Social Interactions and Group Behavior	Systems and System Models
	3	Develop models to describe that organisms have unique and diverse life cycles but all have in common, birth, growth, reproduction, and death.	Developing and Using Models	Growth and Development of Organisms	Patterns
	4	Develop models to describe that organisms have unique and diverse life cycles but all have in common, birth, growth, reproduction, and death.	Developing and Using Models	Growth and Development of Organisms	Patterns

Standards Correlations *(cont.)*

Unit	Week	Performance Expectation	Science and Engineering Practices	Disciplinary Core Ideas	Cross-Cutting Concepts
		Next Generation Science Standards			
Life Science	5	Analyze and interpret data from fossils to provide evidence of the organisms and the environments in which they lived long ago.	Analyzing and Interpreting Data	Evidence of Common Ancestry and Diversity	Scale, Proportion, and Quantity
	6	Analyze and interpret data from fossils to provide evidence of the organisms and the environments in which they lived long ago.	Analyzing and Interpreting Data	Evidence of Common Ancestry and Diversity	Scale, Proportion, and Quantity
	7	Construct an argument with evidence that in a particular habitat some organisms can survive well, some survive less well, and some cannot survive at all.	Engaging in Argument from Evidence	Adaptation	Systems and System Models
	8	Construct an argument with evidence that in a particular habitat some organisms can survive well, some survive less well, and some cannot survive at all.	Engaging in Argument from Evidence	Adaptation	Systems and System Models
	9	Analyze and interpret data to provide evidence that plants and animals have traits inherited from parents and that variation of these traits exists in a group of similar organisms.	Analyzing and Interpreting Data	Inheritance of Traits	Patterns
	10	Use evidence to support the explanation that traits can be influenced by the environment.	Constructing Explanations and Designing Solutions	Inheritance of Traits	Cause and Effect
	11	Use evidence to construct an explanation for how the variations in characteristics among individuals of the same species may provide advantages in surviving, finding mates, and reproducing.	Constructing Explanations and Designing Solutions	Variation of Traits Natural Selection	Cause and Effect
	12	Make a claim about the merit of a solution to a problem caused when the environment changes and the types of plants and animals that live there may change.	Engaging in Argument from Evidence	Ecosystems Dynamics, Functioning, and Resilience Biodiversity and Humans	Systems and System Models
Physical Science	1	Plan and conduct an investigation to provide evidence of the effects of balanced and unbalanced motion of an object.	Planning and Carrying Out Investigations	Forces and Motion	Cause and Effect
	2	Plan and conduct an investigation to provide evidence of the effects of balanced and unbalanced motion of an object.	Planning and Carrying Out Investigations	Forces and Motion	Cause and Effect

Standards Correlations *(cont.)*

Unit	Week	Performance Expectation	Science and Engineering Practices	Disciplinary Core Ideas	Cross-Cutting Concepts
		Next Generation Science Standards			
Physical Science	3	Plan and conduct an investigation to provide evidence of the effects of balanced and unbalanced motion of an object.	Planning and Carrying Out Investigations	Forces and Motion	Cause and Effect
	4	Make observations and/or measurements of an object's motion to provide evidence that a pattern can be used to predict future motion.	Planning and Carrying Out Investigations	Forces and Motion	Patterns
	5	Make observations and/or measurements of an object's motion to provide evidence that a pattern can be used to predict future motion.	Planning and Carrying Out Investigations	Forces and Motion	Patterns
	6	Make observations and/or measurements of an object's motion to provide evidence that a pattern can be used to predict future motion.	Planning and Carrying Out Investigations	Forces and Motion	Patterns
	7	Ask questions to determine cause and effect relationships of electric or magnetic interactions between two objects not in contact with each other.	Asking Questions and Defining Problems	Types of Interactions	Cause and Effect
	8	Ask questions to determine cause and effect relationships of electric or magnetic interactions between two objects not in contact with each other.	Asking Questions and Defining Problems	Types of Interactions	Cause and Effect
	9	Ask questions to determine cause and effect relationships of electric or magnetic interactions between two objects not in contact with each other.	Asking Questions and Defining Problems	Types of Interactions	Cause and Effect
	10	Ask questions to determine cause and effect relationships of electric or magnetic interactions between two objects not in contact with each other.	Asking Questions and Defining Problems	Types of Interactions	Cause and Effect
	11	Define a simple design problem that can be solved by applying scientific ideas about magnets.	Asking Questions and Defining Problems	Types of Interactions	Interdependence of Science, Engineering, and Technology
	12	Define a simple design problem that can be solved by applying scientific ideas about magnets.	Asking Questions and Defining Problems	Types of Interactions	Interdependence of Science, Engineering, and Technology
Earth and Space Science	1	Represent data in tables and graphical displays to describe typical weather conditions expected during a particular season.	Analyzing and Interpreting Data	Weather and Climate	Patterns / Science is a Human Endeavor
	2	Represent data in tables and graphical displays to describe typical weather conditions expected during a particular season.	Analyzing and Interpreting Data	Weather and Climate	Patterns / Science is a Human Endeavor

Standards Correlations (cont.)

| Unit | Week | Next Generation Science Standards | | | |
		Performance Expectation	Science and Engineering Practices	Disciplinary Core Ideas	Cross-Cutting Concepts
Earth and Space Science	3	Represent data in tables and graphical displays to describe typical weather conditions expected during a particular season.	Analyzing and Interpreting Data	Weather and Climate	Patterns Science is a Human Endeavor
	4	Represent data in tables and graphical displays to describe typical weather conditions expected during a particular season.	Analyzing and Interpreting Data	Weather and Climate	Patterns Science is a Human Endeavor
	5	Obtain and combine information to describe climates in different regions of the world.	Obtaining, Evaluating, and Communication Information	Weather and Climate	Patterns
	6	Obtain and combine information to describe climates in different regions of the world.	Obtaining, Evaluating, and Communication Information	Weather and Climate	Patterns
	7	Obtain and combine information to describe climates in different regions of the world.	Obtaining, Evaluating, and Communication Information	The Universe and Its Stars	Patterns
	8	Obtain and combine information to describe climates in different regions of the world.	Obtaining, Evaluating, and Communication Information	The Universe and Its Stars	Patterns
	9	Make a claim about the merit of a design solution that reduces the impacts of a weather-related hazard.	Engaging in Argument from Evidence	The Universe and Its Stars	Influence of Engineering, Technology, and Science on Society and the Natural World Science is a Human Endeavor
	10	Make a claim about the merit of a design solution that reduces the impacts of a weather-related hazard.	Engaging in Argument from Evidence	The Universe and Its Stars	Influence of Engineering, Technology, and Science on Society and the Natural World Science is a Human Endeavor
	11	Make a claim about the merit of a design solution that reduces the impacts of a weather-related hazard.	Engaging in Argument from Evidence	The Universe and Its Stars	Influence of Engineering, Technology, and Science on Society and the Natural World Science is a Human Endeavor
	12	Make a claim about the merit of a design solution that reduces the impacts of a weather-related hazard.	Engaging in Argument from Evidence	The Universe and Its Stars	Influence of Engineering, Technology, and Science on Society and the Natural World Science is a Human Endeavor

Name: _____ **Date:** _____

Directions: Read the text, and answer the questions.

All for One and One for All

Many animals live in groups. There are many reasons for this. They live in groups for safety. They live in groups to help each other care for young. Some animals will watch for predators while others eat. Some grown-up animals live with their young to keep them safe and teach them. Some animals hunt together. This helps the whole group get enough food. Living in a group helps animals.

1. Why do some animals live in groups?

   a. to help each other care for young

   b. for safety

   c. to hunt together

   d. all of the above

2. All animals in a group _____ .

   a. sleep at the same time

   b. are the same age

   c. eat at the same time

   d. help each other

3. What might happen if an animal got separated from its group?

   It Might get eaten.

   _____

   _____

Name: _____ Date: _____

Directions: Names are given to different groups of animals. Study the pictures, and answer the questions.

gaggle of geese

herd of elephants

school of fish

sounder of pigs

pride of lions

herd of deer

Analyzing Data

1. Groups of animals _____ .

    a. always have the same name

    b. always have the same number of animals in each group

    c. sometimes have the same name

    d. have names that tell where they live

2. What is a group of lions called?

    a. herd

    b. sounder

    c. school

    d. pride

3. Why is it helpful to have special names for groups of animals?

    _____

    _____

Developing Questions

Name: _____ **Date:** _____

Directions: Read the text, and answer the questions.

A group of lions is called a pride. Prides have lions of all ages in them. There are usually two or three adult males in a pride and up to 12 females. They do not let lions who aren't part of the group live with them.

While on safari, you see 10 lions. There are two adult males and seven females huddled together. Another adult male is walking toward the group. The two males in the group are roaring. You want to know if these lions make up a pride.

1. What question would help you decide if the lions are a pride?

    a. Do any of the lions seem like they don't belong?

    b. Are the lions playing?

    c. Are the lions sleeping?

    d. Are the lions young?

2. What might happen if a lion who doesn't belong tries to join a pride?

    a. The females will welcome the lion.

    b. The males will attack the lion.

    c. The babies will play with the lion.

    d. They will share food with the new lion.

3. Write a question you have about prides of lions.

_____

_____

_____

Name: _____ **Date:** _____

Directions: Read the text, and answer the questions.

Philip has a bowl with two goldfish. He gets a new goldfish. He wants all of his fish to live together. He decides to put the new goldfish in the same bowl with his other fish.

1. How can Philip tell if the first two fish will live with the new fish?

   a. He can watch to see if they ignore the new fish.

   b. He can watch to see if they attack the new fish.

   c. He can watch to see if they swim with the new fish.

   d. All of the above.

2. Why would Philip put the same kinds of fish together?

   a. They might not like other kinds of fish.

   b. Other fish might not eat the same kinds of food.

   c. It would be hard to find another kind of fish.

   d. both a and b

3. How could Philip test to see if the goldfish would accept another kind of fish in the bowl?

   _____

   _____

   _____

Planning Solutions

Communicating Results

Name: _____ **Date:** _____

Directions: The box lists the number of animals a scientist observed for each group. Use the information to complete the graph. Then, answer the question.

baboons: 68	killer whales: 40
lions: 15	zebras: 20
elephants: 100	

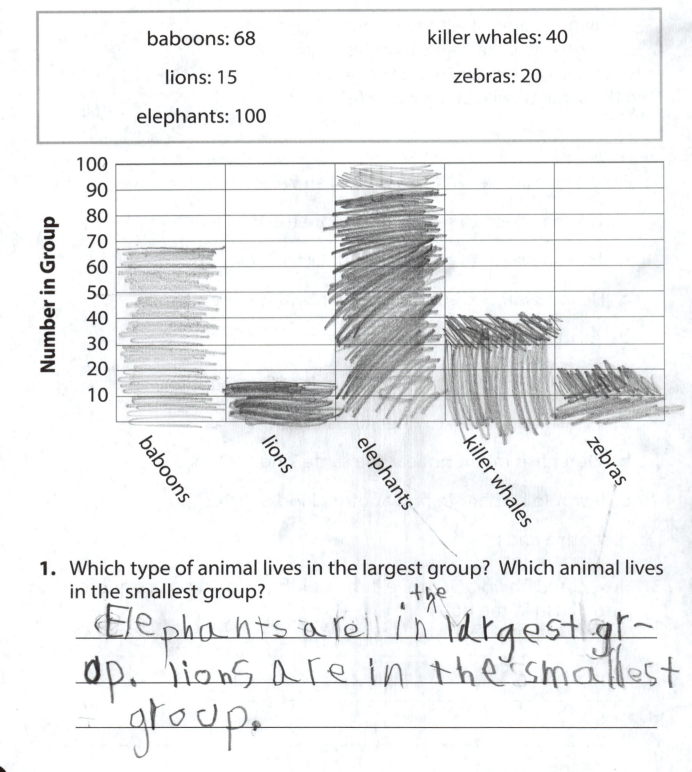

1. Which type of animal lives in the largest group? Which animal lives in the smallest group?

   Elephants are in the largest gr-
   op. lions are in the smallest
   group.

Name: _____ **Date:** _____

Directions: Read the text, and answer the questions.

What's Your Job?

Each animal in a group has a job. These jobs help the whole group. One job is to get food. Usually, both males and females can do this, but sometimes one gender does it more than the other. Another job of animals is to help each other stay clean. This is called grooming. Both males and females groom. Sometimes males and females have different jobs. Females give birth and often raise young, and males often protect the group from other males.

1. What is one job male animals often have?

   a. protecting the group

   b. getting food

   c. raising babies

   d. grooming

2. What job do females have that males can't do?

   a. giving birth

   b. grooming

   c. hunting

   d. protecting the group

3. Why might both male and female animals hunt?

   _____

   _____

Name: _____ **Date:** _____

Directions: Males and females can have different jobs. Study the chart. Answer the questions.

	Female Baboon	Male Baboon
gets food	X	X
has a baby	X	
fights enemies		X
watches for danger	X	X
grooms others	X	X

1. What do male baboons do that female baboons don't do?

   a. share food

   b. groom other baboons

   c. get food

   d. fight enemies

2. Why might it be harder for female baboons to defend the troop?

   a. They spend more time grooming.

   b. They have babies to take care of.

   c. They need more food to eat.

   d. They don't run as fast.

3. What is the benefit of both males and females getting food?

   _____

   _____

Name: _____ Date: _____

Directions: Read the text, and answer the questions.

Some animals stand in a circle. Stronger animals stand on the outside of the circle, and weaker animals stand inside the circle.

1. What animals stand on the outside of the circle?

   a. baby animals

   b. sick animals

   c. old animals

   d. strong animals

2. Why might the weaker animals stand inside the circle?

   a. for protection

   b. for grooming

   c. to eat

   d. for hunting

3. What could you ask about animals that stand in circles?

   _____

   _____

Planning Solutions

Name: _____ **Date:** _____

Directions: Make up an imaginary animal. Its job is to protect animals in its group. Answer the questions.

1. To do its job, your animal needs to be _____ .

   a. strong   **b.** colorful

   c. slow   **d.** noisy

2. If your animal had to defend the group at night, it would need _____ .

   a. large ears   **b.** big paws

   c. good night vision   **d.** a long tail

3. What else should your animal have?

   Whiskers _____

   _____

4. Draw a picture of your imaginary animal.

Name: _____ Date: _____

Directions: Read the text. Then, draw and label the animals where they would be found in the circle.

> A herd of musk ox is protecting itself from a wolf. There are four adult oxen, three young oxen, and two baby oxen. The wolf isn't afraid of the babies or the young oxen.

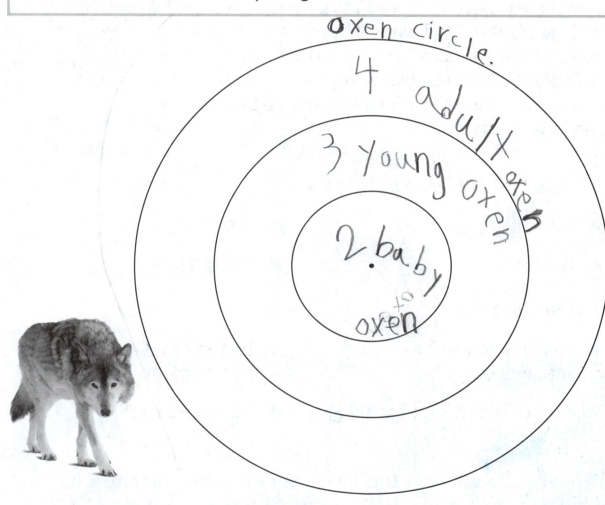

oxen circle.
4 adult oxen
3 young oxen
2. baby oxen

1. How did you decide which ox should be on the inside of the circle?

The 2 babys are the weakist
(Sorry babys)

_____

Name: _____ **Date:** _____

Directions: Read the text, and answer the questions.

Learning Content

Life Cycle of Plants

Flowering plants have similar life cycles. They begin as seeds that *germinate*, or start to grow. Then they develop into seedlings. Seedlings become plants with flowers that produce new seeds. The seeds fall to the ground and make more plants. The new plants will be the same kind as their parent. They will also make their own new plants.

1. What is the next stage *after* the seed?

   a. new plant

   b. seedling

   c. flower

   d. mature plant

2. A new plant will _____ .

   a. make seeds before it flowers

   b. be the same kind as its parent plant

   c. be a different kind than its parent

   d. become a seedling

3. Why would a young plant live in the same environment as its parent plant?

   _____It's the same plant._____

   _____

   _____

Name: _____ **Date:** _____

Directions: Study the picture of a life cycle of a tomato plant. Then, answer the questions.

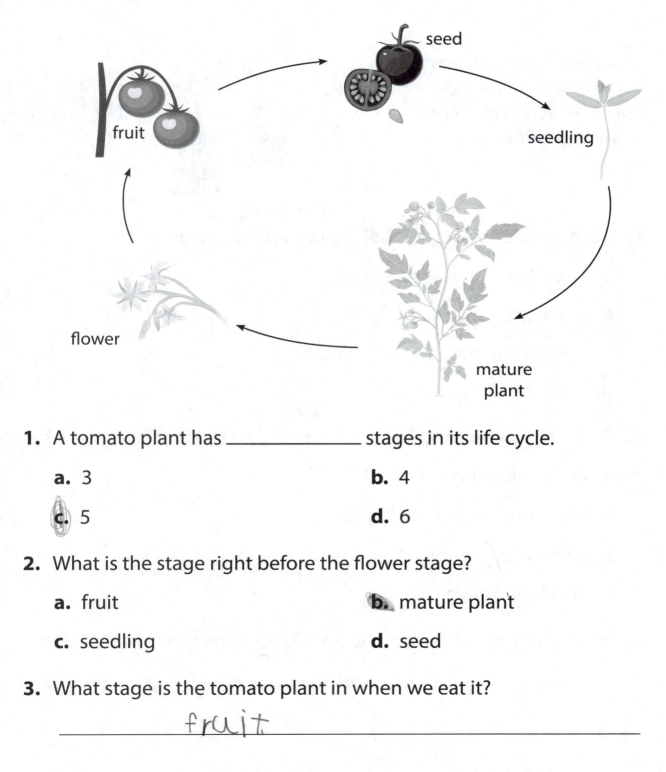

1. A tomato plant has _____ stages in its life cycle.

   a. 3   **b.** 4

   c. 5   **d.** 6

2. What is the stage right before the flower stage?

   a. fruit   **b.** mature plant

   c. seedling   **d.** seed

3. What stage is the tomato plant in when we eat it?

   _____ fruit _____

   _____

Name: _____ Date: _____

Directions: Read the text, and answer the questions.

> Marla has two tomato plants. The first plant has flower buds on it. The second plant doesn't have any flower buds.

1. What do the flower buds tell Marla about that plant?

   a. It will have tomatoes first.

   b. It will grow faster.

   c. It will need more water.

   d. It will need more sun.

2. Which question could you ask about the plant with flower buds?

   a. How much sun did it get?

   b. How much water did it get?

   c. When was it planted?

   d. All of the above.

3. What could you ask about the flower buds and tomatoes?

   _____

   _____

51409—180 Days of Science

Name: _____ **Date:** _____

Directions: Read the text, and look at the chart. Answer the questions.

> All tomatoes follow the same life cycle. Some grow faster. Some grow slower. This chart shows how different kinds of tomatoes grow.

	Days to Harvest	Size of Plant	Shape	Color
Tomato 1	60 days	medium	round	yellow
Tomato 2	75 days	large	oval	orange
Tomato 3	40 days	small	long	red
Tomato 4	80 days	medium	narrow	striped

1. How can you tell which tomato will be ready to eat the earliest?

    a. by its size   **b.** by its harvest time

    c. by its color   **d.** by its shape

2. You want to have ripe tomatoes all summer. You should _____.

    a. water some a lot   **b.** plant different kinds

    c. feed some to the birds   **d.** plant some in shade

3. You want tomatoes all summer. You only like one kind, though. What should you do?

    _____

    _____

Name: _____ **Date:** _____

Directions: Read Jorge's notes about his garden. Then complete the chart, and answer the question.

> The seeds on the left side of the garden get lots of sun every day. The seeds sprout in three days. The seedlings are bright green. At the end of the month, the plants are five inches tall.
>
> The seeds on the right side of the garden only get sun for a few hours in the afternoon. These seeds sprout in five days. The seedlings are pale green. At the end of the month, the plants are three inches tall.

	Seeds on the Left (Sunny Side)	Seeds on the Right (Shady Side)
time to sprout	3 Days	5 Days
color of seedlings	bright green	pale green
plant's size at the end of the month	5 inches	3 inches

1. What do you think caused the difference between the two sides of the garden? Why?

_____

_____

_____

Name: _____ Date: _____

Directions: Read the text, and answer the questions.

Life Cycle of Animals

All animals go through stages as they grow. Humans do, too. This is called the life cycle. Most animals begin life as a baby. Then they grow into a juvenile, or young animal. The young animal becomes an adult. The adult has babies. Then the life cycle starts over.

1. A life cycle _____ .

   a. is the stages of growth of an animal

   b. starts when you become an adult

   c. is the daily life of an animal

   d. all of the above

2. When does the life cycle start over?

   a. when an adult has a baby

   b. when a juvenile becomes an adult

   c. when a baby becomes a juvenile

   d. when an animal gets too old

3. What are the stages of the life cycle of a human?

   _____

   _____

Analyzing Data

Name: _____ **Date:** _____

Directions: Read the text, and study the two life cycles. Then, answer the questions.

Some baby animals look a lot like their parents. They look like small adults. Some baby animals don't look like adults at all.

1. What part of the life cycle do dogs and frogs have in common?

   a. both live in water as babies   **b.** both become adults

   c. both are born without legs   **d.** both lose their tails

2. How can you tell when a puppy becomes a juvenile?

   a. by how big it is ?   **b.** by what color it is

   c. by how loud it barks   **d.** by how furry its tail is

3. Which animal do you think stays with its mother after it is born? Why?

   _____

   _____

   _____

Name: _____ **Date:** _____

Directions: Read the text, and answer the questions.

> A sea turtle comes out of the ocean. She crawls onto the beach and digs a deep hole. She covers the hole with sand. She goes back into the ocean and swims out to sea. About four months later, small turtles come out of the sand, and they crawl into the ocean.

1. In what stage of the life cycle is the female turtle?

   a. egg

   b. baby

   c. juvenile

   d. adult

2. What is the female turtle doing when she digs the hole?

   a. taking a nap

   b. laying eggs

   c. hiding food

   d. making a home

3. Write a question you have about the way a mother turtle acts with her babies.

   _____

   _____

   _____

   _____

Planning Solutions

Name: _____ **Date:** _____

Directions: Read the text, and answer the questions.

> A zoo gets a new alligator. Adult alligators are 7 to 14 feet long. This alligator is 10 feet long. Alligators can keep growing their whole life. How big they get depends on how much food they eat. It also depends on how much space they have.

1. How can the zookeeper know right now if the alligator is a juvenile or an adult?

   a. by its weight

   b. by its length

   c. by what it eats

   d. she can't know.

2. When the alligator is fully grown, what does the zookeeper have to do?

   a. put the alligator in a smaller tank

   b. make sure the alligator gets enough food

   c. make sure the alligator has enough space

   d. both a and c

3. How can the zookeeper find out how the size of the exhibit affects the size of the alligator?

   _____

   _____

   _____

Name: _____ **Date:** _____

Directions: Read the text, and study the picture. Then, answer the questions.

> Sandy studies fossils. She finds some new fossils. This picture shows what Sandy found.
>
>

1. What is the first thing Sandy needs to know to identify this fossil?

   a. if the fossil is a plant or animal

   b. the age of the creature when it formed the fossil

   c. the habitat where the fossil was found

   d. how many fossils were found

2. What can Sandy do to tell if this is a fossil or just a piece of rock?

   a. She can weigh it.

   b. She can compare it to other fossils.

   c. She can break it apart.

   d. She can measure it.

3. What could Sandy look at to help her decide where this animal lived?

   _____ did it have fins? _____

   _____

Name: _____ **Date:** _____

Directions: Fossils take at least 10,000 years to form. Read the text. Put the steps in the proper order to show how fossils are made.

Communicating Results

Sand and sediments make layers.

A fish dies.

Bones turn to stone.

Its body sinks to bottom of the water.

Mud covers the bones.

Soft parts rot.

How a Fish Fossil Forms

A fish dies

↓

Its body sinks to the bottom of the water

↓

Soft parts rot

↓

Mud covers the bones

↓

Bones turn to stone

↓

Sand and sedimens make layers

Name: _____ **Date:** _____

Directions: Look at the picture. Read the text, and answer the questions.

Fossils

Some scientists study fossils. These are the remains of plants or animals that lived long ago. Sometimes the bones of animals turn to rock. Sometimes molds are made of plants or animals. They also study living things, too. This helps them learn more about the plants and animals that lived long ago.

Learning Content

1. What can you tell by looking at the picture?

   a. how the animal moved

   b. the color of the animal

   c. the lifespan of the animal

   d. how the animal communicated

2. Which part of the animal gives the biggest clue about where it lived?

   a. its mouth

   b. its scales

   c. its fins

   d. its size

3. Would comparing this fossil to living things help the scientist learn more?

   a. Yes, it looks similar to fish that live now.

   b. No, it is unlike any other creature alive now.

   c. Yes, the fossil has scales like living fish.

   d. No, fossils have nothing in common with living things.

Analyzing Data

Name: _____ **Date:** _____

Directions: Study the pictures, and answer the questions.

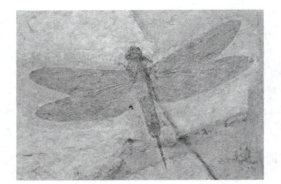 

1. What can you tell from these fossils?

   a. the reason each creature died

   b. if the animals were the same

   c. which creature lived longer

   d. the kind of food each creature ate

2. These fossils _____ .

   a. are the actual animal

   b. show how the animal died

   c. show how colorful each creature was

   d. are molds made by the bodies of the creatures

3. What animals do these fossils remind you of?

   _____

   _____

   _____

Name: _____ **Date:** _____

Directions: Read the text, and answer the questions.

Some animals that lived long ago are now gone. We can study fossils of some of these animals.

1. A scientist finds a fish fossil. What might she find nearby?

   a. more fish fossils

   b. fossils of other water animals

   c. fossils of plants that lived in water

   d. any of the above

2. What do fossils tell us?

   a. why the animal died

   b. how many animals were alive

   c. what the animals looked like

   d. how the animals made sounds

3. What question could you ask about a fossil?

   _____

   _____

   _____

Planning Solutions

Name: _____ **Date:** _____

Directions: Read the text, and answer the questions.

> Your teacher gives you a picture of a fossil. You have to find a living thing that's like your fossil.

1. What would help you find a similar living thing?

    a. knowing how old the fossil is

    b. knowing when the fossil was found

    c. knowing how long it took to dig up the fossil

    d. knowing the kind of habitat where the creature lived

2. The fossil is most like _____ .

    a. a shell

    b. a dog

    c. a lizard

    d. a dragonfly

3. Make a plan to find a similar living thing.

    _____

    _____

    _____

Name: _____ **Date:** _____

Directions: Look at the pictures. Where the circles overlap, write how they are the same. Write what is different about Fossil #1 on the left. Write what is different about Fossil #2 on the right.

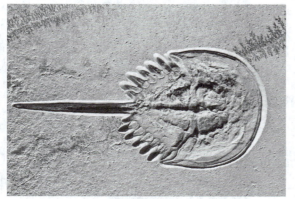

Fossil #1

Fossil #2

Fossil #1   **Fossil #2**

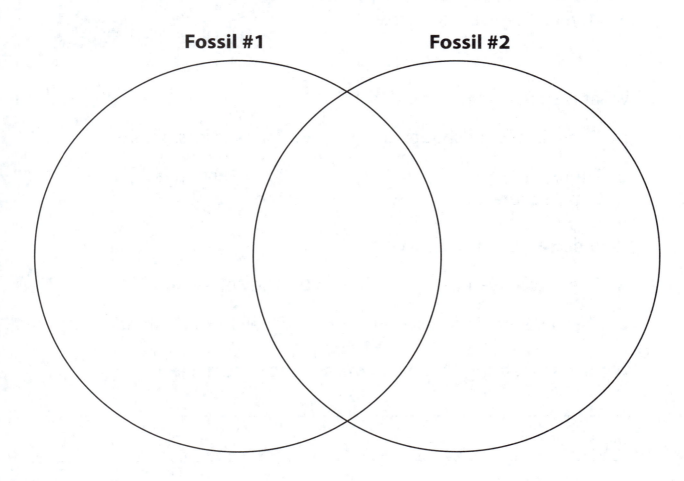

Learning Content

Name: _____   Date: _____

Directions: Read the text, and answer the questions.

Super Survivors

The desert is a very dry place. There is not a lot of rain. It can also be very hot during the day and cooler at night.

A cactus is a desert plant. It is thick and waxy, which helps it store as much water as possible. Desert animals are quiet during the day and more active at night. Each of these things helps plants and animals survive in the desert.

1. What is special about the desert?

   a. There is a lot of shade.

   b. There is lots of rain.

   c. There are high temperatures.

   d. There are always tall mountains.

2. How do cactus plants survive?

   a. They store water.

   b. They eat animals.

   c. They live in rain forests.

   d. They hunt at night.

3. What is something that all animals in the desert need?

   _____

   _____

   _____

Name: _____ **Date:** _____

Directions: Animals have traits, or special features, that help them survive. Study the chart, and answer the questions.

Animal	Trait	Purpose
fennec fox	large ears	help the fox stay cool
fish	gills	help the fish breathe underwater
penguin	thick layer of fat	helps the penguin stay warm
mountain goat	oval, rubber-like hooves	help the goat grip rocks to climb

1. Why are these traits helpful?

   a. They make an animal look nice.

   b. They help animals survive where they live.

   c. They make animals easier to catch.

   d. They help an animal find a new home.

2. Where would the fennec fox's large ears be helpful?

   a. the Arctic

   b. the forest

   c. the ocean

   d. the desert

3. What would happen if the penguin did not have the thick layer of fat?

   a. The penguin couldn't swim.

   b. The penguin would freeze.

   c. The penguin couldn't eat.

   d. The penguin couldn't walk.

Analyzing Data

Name: _____ **Date:** _____

Directions: Read the text, and answer the questions.

> The way an animal can blend in with its surroundings is called camouflage. The Arctic fox has a white coat of fur during the winter months. In the summer, the Arctic fox grows a new coat of fur that is grey and brown.

1. How do you know the Artic fox's fur is a type of camouflage?

   a. The fur does not change with each season.

   b. The fur color makes it stand out.

   c. The white fur would blend in with the snow during the winter.

   d. The fox changes its fur color as it becomes an adult.

2. What question would you ask to decide if an animal is using camouflage?

   a. Is the animal easily seen in its surroundings?

   b. Does the animal move from place to place?

   c. Is the animal able to easily find food to eat?

   d. Does the animal look different from other animals?

3. Write a question you might ask about how animals use camouflage.

   how do animals use camou-

   flage?

Name: _____ **Date:** _____

Directions: Read the text, and answer the questions.

> You are making up an animal. This animal needs to be able to survive in a place that gets a lot of rain. It also has to survive hot summers and cold winters.

Planning Solutions

1. What trait could help your animal survive in the rain?

   a. waterproof feathers, like a duck

   b. thick fur, like a bear

   c. spots, like a leopard

   d. claws, like a hawk

2. How could your animal survive the hot summers?

   a. It could blend in with its surroundings.

   b. It could hunt at night when it is cooler.

   c. It could climb up the tallest trees.

   d. It could have a good sense of hearing.

3. Explain the traits that you would give your imaginary animal, and why.

   _____

   _____

   _____

   _____

Communicating Results

ABC

Name: _____ **Date:** _____

Directions: Match each animal with its trait.

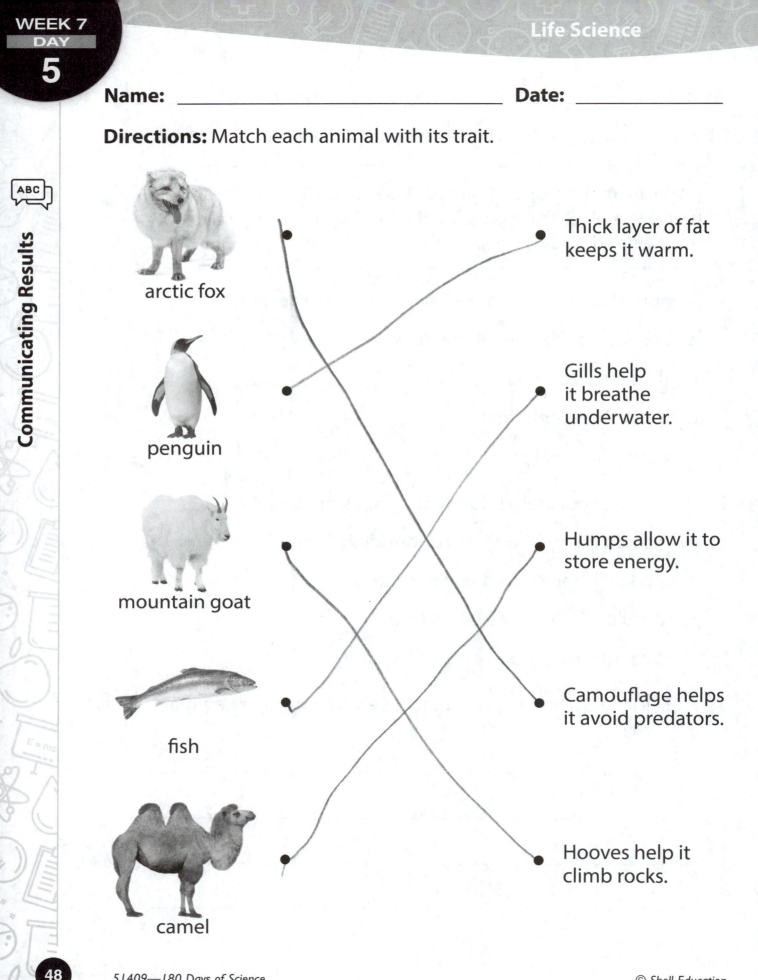

arctic fox

penguin

mountain goat

fish

camel

Thick layer of fat keeps it warm.

Gills help it breathe underwater.

Humps allow it to store energy.

Camouflage helps it avoid predators.

Hooves help it climb rocks.

Name: _____ **Date:** _____

Directions: Read the text, and answer the questions.

Living in a Habitat

Plants and animals need their habitats to live. This is where they get food, water, and shelter. Sometimes humans change the places plants and animals live. Then they no longer have everything they need. A raccoon might be able to find food in a city garbage can. It might not be able to find shelter, though. A forest would give a raccoon everything it needs.

1. Which is a raccoon's natural habitat?

   a. a city garbage can   **b.** a school playground

   c. a parking lot   **d.** a forest

2. What can harm an animal's habitat?

   a. humans   **b.** sunshine

   c. rain   **d.** air

3. Can animals survive out of their habitat?

   a. Yes, but it can be difficult for it to find what it needs.   **b.** No, they can never survive outside of their habitat.

   c. Yes, animals can find what they need anywhere.   **d.** No, not unless they are adopted by humans.

Analyzing Data

Name: _____ **Date:** _____

Directions: Habitats can change with the seasons. These changes affect the plants and animals. This chart shows some changes to a forest summer and in winter. Study the chart, and answer the questions.

Summer	Winter
river water flows	river water freezes
trees are full of leaves	most trees lose leaves
rainfall	snow
insects are active	insects die, migrate, or shelter because it is colder

1. What happens in the winter?

   a. Rivers freeze.   **b.** Insects are active.

   c. Trees have leaves.   **d.** It rains.

2. What would make it harder for an animal to find water in the winter?

   a. frozen rivers   **b.** trees lose leaves

   c. insects die   **d.** fewer hours of daylight

3. Why do some insects migrate in winter?

   a. because the rivers melt   **b.** because the food supply
   and flow   becomes plentiful

   c. because winter brings   **d.** because trees are full
   colder temperatures   of leaves

Name: _____ **Date:** _____

Directions: Read the text, and answer the questions.

> Light is very important to sea turtles. Baby sea turtles use the light of the moon to find the ocean. The moonlight reflecting off the ocean should be the brightest thing. When humans build buildings on the beach, artificial light can confuse the turtles. They don't know which way to go.

1. How would building on the beach affect the sea turtles?

   a. It would give the baby sea turtles more food.

   b. It would increase places for nests.

   c. It would provide more warmth for the eggs in the sand.

   d. It would make it difficult for the babies to get to the ocean.

2. Why do baby sea turtles get confused when going to the ocean?

   a. They follow the building lights instead of the moonlight.

   b. The buildings destroy habitats for predators.

   c. The baby sea turtles have to travel further to the ocean.

   d. There are more babies that have to get to the ocean.

3. What question can you ask about helping the sea turtles?
   can we turn the lights of?
   _____

Planning Solutions

Name: _____ **Date:** _____

Directions: Read the text, and answer the questions.

> Selena notices some ducks in a pond near the school. There is a sign that says, "Please do not feed the ducks." Selena wonders why.

1. Why might it be harmful to feed the ducks?

    a. It can pollute the water.

    b. It can attract more ducks than the habitat can support.

    c. both a and b

    d. none of the above

2. What would tell you if the ducks are surviving well in the pond?

    a. checking the health of the ducks

    b. measuring the amount of water

    c. tallying the number of trees

    d. recording the amount of sunlight

3. What would be the next step that Selena could take to see if the ducks are surviving well?

    _____

    _____

    _____

Name: _____ **Date:** _____

Directions: Read the text, and study the diagram. Answer the questions.

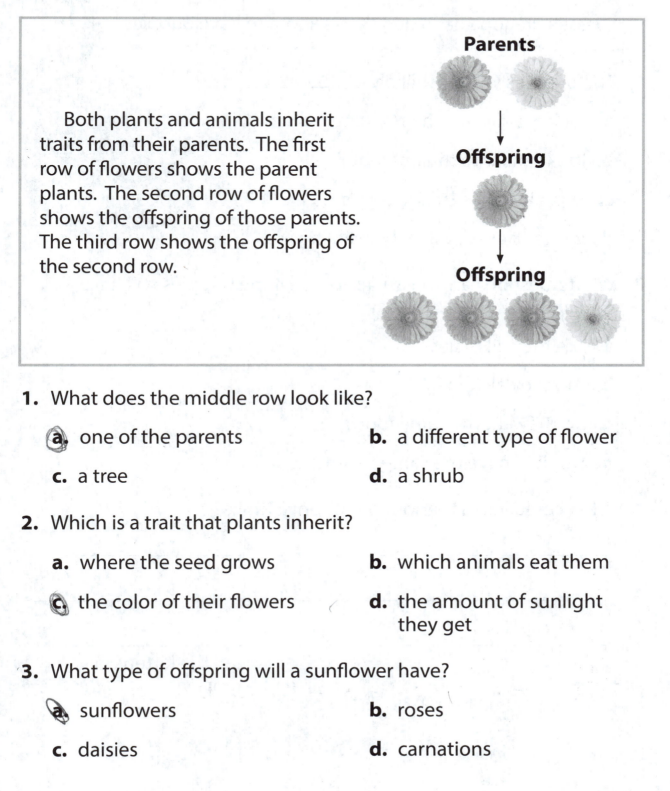

Both plants and animals inherit traits from their parents. The first row of flowers shows the parent plants. The second row of flowers shows the offspring of those parents. The third row shows the offspring of the second row.

Parents

Offspring

Offspring

1. What does the middle row look like?

   a. one of the parents   b. a different type of flower

   c. a tree   d. a shrub

2. Which is a trait that plants inherit?

   a. where the seed grows   b. which animals eat them

   c. the color of their flowers   d. the amount of sunlight they get

3. What type of offspring will a sunflower have?

   a. sunflowers   b. roses

   c. daisies   d. carnations

Developing Questions

Name: _____ **Date:** _____

Directions: Read the text, and answer the questions.

> Jesse's grandpa has a dog that is about to have puppies.

1. The puppies will most likely _____ .

   a. look exactly like their parents

   b. look similar to their parents

   c. won't look like their parents

   d. will look exactly like their siblings

2. What question can you ask to decide if the puppies will have similar traits?

   a. Are they all males?

   b. Are they all females?

   c. Do they eat the same food?

   d. Do they have the same parents?

3. What could you ask about the puppies' traits?

   _____

   _____

   _____

Name: _____ **Date:** _____

Directions: Read the text, and answer the questions.

> Aiden collects some seeds from one plant. The plant has red flowers. He wants to find out if the seeds will grow into plants that look like the parent plant.

1. Aiden plants the seeds. What color flowers should he expect the new plants to have?

   a. blue

   b. red

   c. white

   d. yellow

2. How can Aiden compare the new plants to the parent plants?

   a. Measure the height of both plants when they are mature.

   b. Look at the plants around them.

   c. Write down how much water they get.

   d. Write down how much sunlight they get.

3. How else can Aiden compare the parent plants to the new plants?

   _____

   _____

   _____

   _____

Planning Solutions

Communicating Results

genes
jeans

Name: _____   **Date:** _____

Directions: Look at the picture. Circle the traits that the woman could pass to her child.

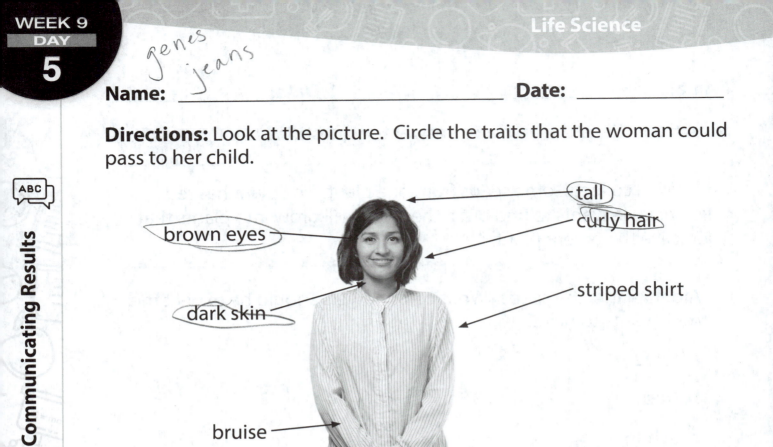

tall

curly hair

brown eyes

striped shirt

dark skin

bruise

1. Will the way the father looks affect how the child looks? Why or why not?

    _____

    _____

    _____

Name: _____   Date: _____

Directions: Read the text, and answer the questions.

Living Things Around Us

Plants and animals are affected by the world around them. Changes can happen that affect how they live. Food sources can change. The amount of available water can change. If humans cut down trees, birds might lose their homes. If one animal dies out, it can change the amount of food available for another animal. Plants and animals try to change to survive.

1. What might happen if trees were cut down in the forest?

   a. Birds lose their homes.

   b. Plants don't get as much sunlight.

   c. Predators struggle with hunting.

   d. The temperature would drop.

2. The food supply is decreasing for a wolf. What might happen?

   a. The wolf will gain weight.

   b. The wolf will lose weight.

   c. The wolf will grow stronger.

   d. The wolf will get less exercise.

3. Why do living things try to change with the environment?

   a. to decrease the number of plants

   b. to change the climate of the habitat

   c. to increase the amount of water

   d. to survive and have offspring

Analyzing Data

Name: _____ **Date:** _____

Directions: Animals and plants can end up where they don't belong. These are called invasive species. They can hurt native species. Native species are what normally live in a certain place.

Invasive Species in Texas	Impact
wild hogs	hurt plants, take food away from other animals
hydrilla	raises water temperature, hurts other water plants
red fire ants	reduce native insects, destroy bird eggs
Africanized bees	hurt almond and melon crops

1. What hurts farmers' crops?

a. red fire ants   b. wild hogs

c. Africanized bees   d. hydrilla

2. What impact might wild hogs have on native animal species?

a. They will increase.   b. They will decrease.

c. They will have more food   d. They will have a better
   than usual.   chance of surviving.

3. Why does it matter that hydrilla raises water temperature?

a. Animals will enjoy the   b. It hurts other water plants.
   warm water.

c. It helps the other plants.   d. It doesn't matter.

Name: _____ **Date:** _____

Directions: Read the text, and answer the questions.

Sea otters live in water. They sometimes eat animals that have shells, like clams. Some sea otters use rocks as a tool. They use the rocks to crack open the shells of animals they eat. Using tools is a learned behavior that helps otters survive.

1. How do rocks help the sea otters?

   a. They allow otters to swim faster.

   b. They help otters groom their fur.

   c. They make it easier for otters to eat the food they need.

   d. They help otters share the food they have.

2. Are otters born knowing how to use rocks as tools?

   a. Yes, they know this when they are born.

   b. No, they learn how to use rocks.

   c. Yes, they learn it before they are born.

   d. No, they don't use rocks as tools.

3. What is a question you could ask about otters using rocks?

   _____

   _____

   _____

Planning Solutions

Name: _____ Date: _____

Directions: Read the text, and look at the chart. Then, answer the questions.

Olivia is studying two plants. She plants the same seeds in identical pots and soil. They are in the same window for sunlight. Each week, she gives 9 mL of water to Plant A and 30 mL of water to Plant B. She compare the plants after three weeks.

	Size	Leaves	Roots
Plant A	small	few	long, thin, and stringy
Plant B	large	many	thick, white, bundled ball of roots

1. Why do Plant A's roots look different?

   a. more hours of sunlight

   b. too much space to grow

   c. not enough water

   d. too much sunlight

2. Why would Olivia use the same kind of plant?

   a. so the flowers could be identical

   b. to compare the same kind of roots

   c. to have the stems be the same color

   d. so that there would be the same number of leaves

3. What could Olivia change about the experiment to see how it affects the plants?

   _____

   _____

Name: _____ **Date:** _____

Directions: Read the statements. Complete the chart to show examples of cause and effect. The first one has been done for you. Then, answer the question.

| Trees are cut down. | An invasive species of insect is introduced. |
| Native species of insects die out. | Squirrels move to a different part of the forest. |

Cause	Effect
There is not enough rain.	Plants start to die.

1. What is another example of cause and effect?

_____

_____

Learning Content

Name: _____ **Date:** _____

Directions: Read the text, and answer the questions.

Variations in Animals

Animals are never exactly the same. There can even be differences in groups of the same kind of animal. These differences are called variations. They can help animals survive. One animal might be able to run faster. One might be better at finding a mate. One might have better vision that makes it easier to find food. All of these things help individual animals.

1. Which is an example of how an animal's variation helps it survive?

   a. It is taller so it can be easily seen.

   b. It has camouflage coloring to blend in.

   c. It is slower to move and escape.

   d. It has worse eyesight to see food.

2. Animals have variations _____ .

   a. that make it easier to tell each other apart

   b. that help them to communicate

   c. that create a brand new species

   d. that make it easier to survive

3. Which is NOT a variation that would help an animal survive?

   a. softer fur

   b. thicker skin

   c. sharper teeth

   d. faster speed

Name: _____ **Date:** _____

Analyzing Data

Directions: These finches have different beaks to eat different foods. Study the pictures of finches and their food. Then, answer the questions.

Large Ground Finch
(seeds)

Cactus Ground Finch
(cactus fruits and flowers)

Vegetarian Finch
(buds)

Woodpecker Finch
(insects)

1. How are the different beaks helpful?

   a. They help each bird get the food it needs.
   b. They are attractive to mates.

   c. They protect the birds.
   d. They help the birds fly.

2. The shape of each beak matches the type of _____ .

   a. water that they drink
   b. nest they live in

   c. weather
   d. food that they eat

3. Birds that eat cactus fruit have a _____ beak.

   a. short, round
   b. curved

   c. longer, sharp
   d. wide

Name: _____ Date: _____

Directions: Read the text, and answer the questions.

Hummingbirds are tiny birds that fly very fast.

1. What is a unique characteristic of this species of bird?

    a. They lay eggs.
    b. They build nests.

    c. They fly quickly.
    d. They have feathers.

2. Which might be a variation in an individual?

    a. the number of birds in an area
    b. the length of its beak

    c. the mate that it chooses
    d. the food that it eats

3. What is a question you can ask to find out more about the variations in hummingbirds?

    _____

    _____

    _____

Name: _____ **Date:** _____

Directions: Read the text, and answer the questions.

> Black-footed ferrets eat prairie dogs. Prairie dogs make up most of their diet. Ferrets use their sharp teeth to capture them. Ferrets are also hunted by other animals.

1. Which variation would help a black-footed ferret catch more prairie dogs?

   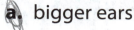 **a.** bigger ears

   b. shorter body

   c. fewer teeth

   d. sharper teeth

2. Which variation would help black-footed ferrets avoid predators?

   a. faster running speed

   b. slower running speed

   c. shorter tails

   d. longer bodies

3. Ferrets are long and slender to fit in prairie dog tunnels. Plan an investigation to study how a variation in size could affect black-footed ferrets.

   _____

   _____

   _____

Planning Solutions

Communicating Results

Name: _____ **Date:** _____

Directions: Draw two of the same kind of animal. One should have a variation. Label the variation. Then, answer the question.

1. Explain what you drew. How could the variation affect the animal?

_____

_____

_____

Name: _____ **Date:** _____

Directions: Read the text, and answer the questions.

Changes for the Better?

Changes to the environment affect everything in it. Temperatures can change. The amount of food and water available can change, too. Changes can come from humans, plants, or animals. Living things must find a way to adapt to these changes. If they can't, they have to find a new place to live. Otherwise, they will die out.

1. What do changes to an environment affect?

   a. plants   **b.** animals

   c. everything   **d.** nothing

2. What must living things do if the environment changes?

   a. eat   **b.** run

   c. jump   **d.** adapt

3. What might happen if an animal can't adapt to changes?

   a. It will die out.   **b.** It will be strong.

   c. More animals will be born. **d.** Nothing will change.

4. What might an animal do if a person cut down the tree it lived in?

   _____

   _____

Analyzing Data

Name: _____   Date: _____

Directions: Read the text. Study the chart. Then, answer the questions.

> Canada geese live in the north during summer. When winter comes, they fly south to warmer climates.

Change	Effect
lakes and ponds freeze	Geese can't swim or dive for food.
temperature drop	Geese cannot survive in the low temperatures.
plants go dormant	Geese don't have enough food.

1. When plants go dormant, _____ .

   a. geese lose a food source

   b. geese have plenty of food

   c. geese don't have nests

   d. geese can't swim

2. Geese fly to areas where _____ .

   a. the lakes aren't frozen

   b. the lakes don't have food

   c. the lakes are frozen

   d. there are no lakes

3. If the winters in Canada became much warmer, do you think the geese would still migrate? Why or why not?

   _____

   _____

   _____

Name: _____ **Date:** _____

Directions: Read the text, and answer the questions.

A red fox eats crickets and beetles. A disease wipes out all of the crickets in the habitat. The crickets and beetles used to compete for food. Now that the crickets are gone, there is more food for the beetles. The beetle population increases because there is no competition for food.

1. What happens to the number of beetles?

   a. It increases because the crickets are gone.

   b. It increases because it is easier to find mates.

   c. It decreases because the foxes don't eat them.

   d. It stays the same.

2. What would bring the number of beetles back to normal?

   a. Figure out where the disease came from.

   b. Introduce crickets back into the habitat to create competition for food.

   c. Decrease the number of foxes so that there are no predators for beetles.

   d. Bring in a new predator for crickets.

3. What can you ask to find out more about what happened to the crickets?

   _____

   _____

   _____

   _____

Planning Solutions

Name: _____ **Date:** _____

Directions: Read the text, and answer the questions.

There are fewer butterflies than the year before. They only eat one type of weed. This weed is disappearing. Derek is teaching his classmates how to plant the weed for the butterflies.

1. Why might there be fewer butterflies?

    a. fewer weeds

    b. fewer predators

    c. higher temperatures

    d. increased habitat space

2. What could help the butterflies survive in their habitat?

    a. create a warmer environment

    b. move them farther away

    c. continue to build near their habitat

    d. plant more of their food

3. What information would Derek need to collect to see if his solution is working?

    _____

    _____

Name: _____ **Date:** _____

Directions: Read the text. Then, answer the questions.

> The soil in a famer's field is starting to wash away with rain. The field is empty. The farmer decides to plant this field to keep the soil in place.

1. Draw and label a picture of the farmer's solution.

2. Do you think the farmer's change was good or bad for the environment? Why?

_____

_____

_____

© Shell Education

Communicating Results

Learning Content

Name: _____ **Date:** _____

Directions: Look at the picture. Read the text, and answer the questions.

Pull, Pull, Pull

Force is something that changes the motion of an object. Pulling is when you use force to move an object toward you. The more force you use, the faster the object moves. It is more difficult to pull an object that is still. It is easier to pull an object when it is already moving toward you.

1. Pulling _____ .

    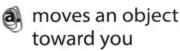 moves an object toward you

    b. moves an object away from you

    c. is always easy

    d. is always hard

2. It is more difficult to pull an object _____ .

    a. that doesn't weigh a lot

    b. that is moving in a different direction

    c. that is already moving in the same direction

    d. when someone else is helping to pull

3. To pull an object, you apply _____ .

    a. no force

    b. friction

    c. a force away from you

    d. a force toward you

Name: _____ **Date:** _____

Directions: Read the text, and study the chart. Then, answer the questions.

> Stefan did an experiment with a bucket of water. He wanted to see how much force it took to pick it up.

Amount of Water	Force Needed
1 liter	low
3 liters	medium
5 liters	high

1. Which amount of water requires the most force to pull?

   a. 1 liter   **b.** 3 liters

   c. 5 liters   **d.** They were all the same.

2. Which amount of water requires the least force to pull?

   a. 1 liter   **b.** 3 liters

   c. 5 liters   **d.** They were all the same.

3. What do you think would happen if Stefan asked a friend to help him lift the bucket?

   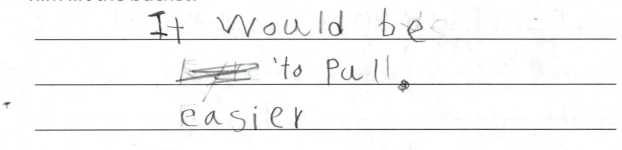

   It would be ~~____~~ to pull. easier

Name: _____ **Date:** _____

Directions: Read the text, and answer the questions.

> Audrey brings her empty wagon outside. She wants to bring some toys to her friend's house. She puts them in her wagon and starts to pull it on the sidewalk.

Developing Questions

1. It is most difficult for Audrey to pull her wagon _____.

   a. before her toys are in it

   b. after her toys are in it

   c. as she is pulling it on the sidewalk

   d. when she takes the toys out at her friend's house

2. Audrey's friend wants a ride in the wagon. When her friend gets in, the wagon _____.

   a. is easier to pull

   b. can go faster

   c. is lighter

   d. is harder to pull

3. What could you ask about pulling Audrey's wagon?

   If your friend gets out will it be easier?

   _____

Name: _____ **Date:** _____

Directions: Look at the picture. Read the text, and answer the questions.

Jeremy and his friends are going sledding on his giant sled. There are five friends including Jeremy, and the sled can hold them all.

Planning Solutions

1. Jeremy is pulling three of his friends on the sled, and they want to go faster. Jeremy should _____.

    a. walk slower

    b. pull with less force

    c. pull with more force

    d. have more friends get on

2. Once the sled is moving, is it easier or harder to pull?

    a. easier

    b. harder

    c. much harder

    d. It is the same.

3. What could Jeremy do to find out more about force and the speed of the sled?

    Pull it to a hill!!!

Name: _____ **Date:** _____

Directions: Study the pictures below. Circle the picture that shows more force required to move the wagon. Then, answer the questions.

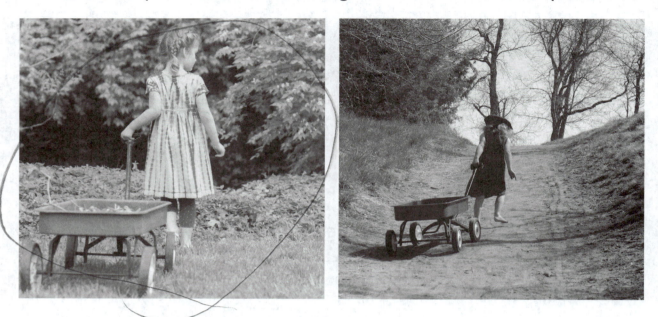

1. Why did you choose the picture you circled?

     Grass, Stuff in wagon

2. What would happen if you added more objects to the wagon in the first picture?

     SLoow

3. If two identical wagons were empty, would they require the same amount of force to pull? Why or why not?

     not if they were on different
     sirfuses (surfaces)

Name: _____ **Date:** _____

Directions: Read the text, and answer the questions.

Get the Ball Rolling

It doesn't take much force to get a ball. The surface that the ball is on may affect how much force is needed to roll the ball. The surface may be rough like wood chips, or it may be smooth like the blacktop on a playground. The surface may be flat, or it may be hilly or angled. The surface and the amount of force used on the ball will affect whether the ball moves quickly or slowly.

1. When will a ball start to roll?

   a. when it is placed in a grassy area

   b. when it is sitting in wood chips

   c. when the ground is flat

   d. when it is pushed

2. What determines how fast the ball will roll?

   a. the surface the ball is on

   b. the color of the ball

   c. the time of day

   d. the temperature

3. Which ball would be hardest to roll?

   a. a basketball on a court

   b. a baseball on a hill

   c. a beach ball in tall grass

   d. a rubber ball on a hard floor

Analyzing Data

Name: _____ **Date:** _____

Directions: Jennifer rolls a ball down the ramp and records how long it takes to reach the bottom. She tries the ramp at three different heights. Look at the chart, and answer the questions.

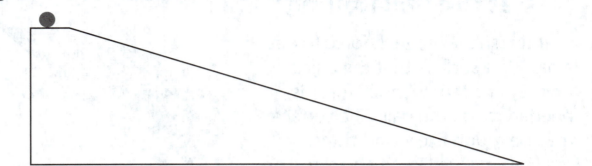

Height of Ramp	Time
5 cm	8 seconds
10 cm	6 seconds
15 cm	4 seconds

1. How high was the ramp when the ball rolled the fastest?

   a. 15 cm   **b.** 5 cm

   c. 10 cm   **d.** flat

2. How high was the ramp when the ball rolled the slowest?

   a. 15 cm   **b.** 19 cm

   c. 5 cm   **d.** flat

3. How does the speed of the ball change with the height of the ramp?

   _____

   _____

   _____

Name: _____   **Date:** _____

Directions: Read the text, and answer the questions.

In soccer, many forces act on a ball. These forces cause the ball to speed up and change direction. They cause them to roll along a surface and stop. Before kicking the ball, players need to know which direction they want it to go. They also need to know how fast they want it to go.

1. How can a player can apply forces to a soccer ball?

   a. kick it

   b. stop it

   c. change its direction

   d. all of the above

2. What MOST determines how a soccer ball travels?

   a. the color of the ball

   b. the size of the ball

   c. how hard the ball is kicked

   d. the team playing in the game

3. Write a question about how kicking affects a soccer ball.

   _____

   _____

   _____

   _____

Planning Solutions

Name: _____ **Date:** _____

Directions: Read the text, and answer the questions.

Sophia is building a snowman in her hilly yard. She is trying to figure out the best place to put the snowman.

1. How will the amount of force Sophia needs to push the snowball change as it gets bigger?

   a. She will need less force.

   b. She will need more force.

   c. She will need the same amount of force.

   d. She will need a lot of force and then less force.

2. How is pushing the snowball up a hill different than pushing it on the flat ground?

   a. It is harder.

   b. It is easier.

   c. It is no different.

   d. The snowball won't move.

3. What could Sophia do to find out how the hills affect the force needed to move the snowballs?

   Push it down a hill.

   Push it up a hill.

   _____

   _____

Name: _____ **Date:** _____

Directions: Study the diagram. Follow the directions, and answer the question.

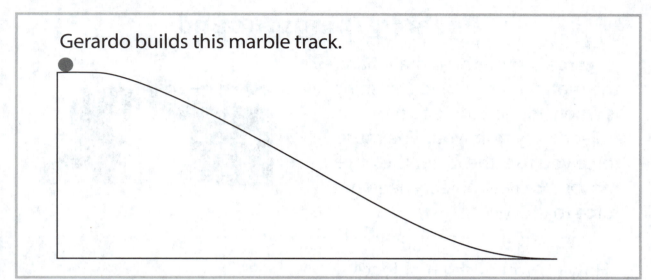

Gerardo builds this marble track.

1. Draw a diagram to show how Gerardo could build a track to make the marble roll faster.

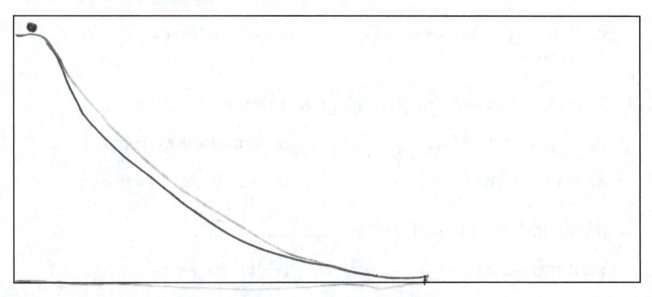

2. Do you think a heavier ball would roll faster or slower? Why?

faster because it is heavier

Communicating Results

Learning Content

Name: _____ Date: _____

Directions: Read the text, and answer the questions.

Pushing Things Around

Force is something that changes the motion of an object. Pushing is when you use force to move an object away from you. The more force you use, the faster the object moves. Heavier objects need more force to move.

1. How do you push an object?

   a. Apply a force towards you.   b. Apply a force away from you.

   c. Pushing does not need a force.   d. Leave the object alone.

2. To make an object move quickly, you should _____.

   a. apply a lot of force   b. apply a little force

   c. don't apply any force   d. add weight to the object

3. If you add weight to the object, _____.

   a. it moves faster   b. it is easier to push

   c. it is more difficult to push   d. it needs less force to push

4. What would be the difference between pushing a box full of books and an empty box?

   The book box is more difficult to push.

Name: _____ **Date:** _____

Directions: Read the text, and study the chart. Then, answer the questions.

> Groceries at the store have different weights. Adding groceries to the grocery cart can affect the force needed to push the cart.

Item	Weight (kg)	Difficulty to Push
box of rice	0.25	easy
can of soup	0.5	easy
cantaloupe	1	medium
a gallon of milk	3.5	medium
a 24-pack of bottled water	11	hard

1. When is it easiest to push the grocery cart?

   a. with milk

   b. with a box of rice

   c. with the bottled water

   d. with a can of soup

2. What happens as items are added to the cart?

   a. The cart gets lighter.

   b. The cart gets easier to push.

   c. There is no change to the cart.

   d. The cart gets more difficult to push.

3. How hard do you think it would be to push the cart if you had five gallons of milk? Why?

   _____ hard _____

   _____

Name: _____ Date: _____

Directions: Read the text, and answer the questions.

A few friends are sledding down a hill. They take turns pushing each other. Each one tries to see who can go the fastest.

1. Which is an important factor in getting the sled to go fast?

   a. the sled's color

   b. the time of day

   c. the amount of sun

   d. using a lot of force to push the sled

2. Which friend can push the sled so that it goes the fastest?

   a. the smartest

   b. the tallest

   c. the strongest

   d. the funniest

3. What can you ask about the force of the push and the speed of the sled?

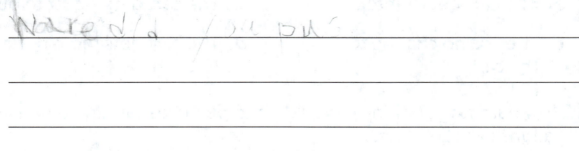

Developing Questions

Name: _____ **Date:** _____

Directions: Read the text, and answer the questions.

Jill is moving. She needs help getting boxes ready for the moving truck. There are many boxes that need to be pushed from one side of the garage to the other. She has some strong friends who offered to help.

1. Which box will be the most difficult to push across the floor?

   a. the lightest

   b. the smallest

   c. the heaviest

   d. the one with wheels

2. If the boxes are the same size, which box would be the most difficult?

   a. a box of tissues

   b. a box of books

   c. a box of board games

   d. a box of shoes

3. What can Jill do to make the boxes easier to move?

   _____

   _____

   _____

   _____

Communicating Results

Name: _____ **Date:** _____

Directions: Mason is moving the same object using different amounts of force. Make a bar graph using the data in the chart. Then, answer the question.

Trial	Distance
1	2.5 meters $2\frac{1}{2}$
2	3 meters
3	1 meter
4	6 meters
5	8 meters

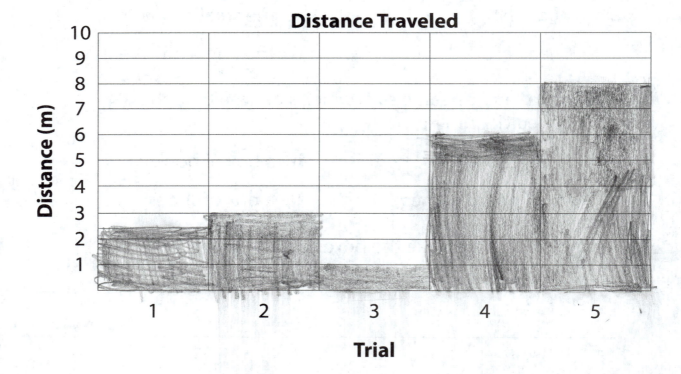

Distance Traveled

1. Based on this data, in which trial did Mason use the greatest force?

_____ 5 _____

_____

Name: _____ **Date:** _____

Directions: Read the text, and answer the questions.

Playing Along

If you have ever ridden a seesaw, you know that it goes up and down. A seesaw is a beam that is balanced in the middle on a support. Force is needed to move the seesaw. Each person on a seesaw has to push off the ground to make his or her side go up. Then the other person does the same thing. If both people put their feet down at the same time, the seesaw will be level.

1. When one person pushes off the ground, his or her side of the seesaw goes _____ .

   a. down   **b.** up

   c. left   **d.** nowhere

2. What is needed to create a level seesaw?

   a. The force on the left should be greater.

   b. The force on the right should be greater.

   c. The forces don't affect whether the beam is level.

   d. The forces on each side should be equal.

3. Which of the following is true about a seesaw that is tilting to the right?

   a. The person on the left pushed off the ground.

   b. The beam is large.

   c. The person on the right pushed off the ground.

   d. The beam is small.

Name: _____ Date: _____

Directions: A seesaw is similar to a scale. Study the chart about a scale. Answer the questions.

Weights on Left	Weights on Right	Direction tilted
500 g	250 g	left
250 g	500 g	right
500 g	500 g	balanced

1. What has to happen for the scale to balance?

   a. equal weight on both sides   b. more weight on the left

   c. more weight on the right   d. twice as much weight on the left

2. If the scale has 500 g on the right, how much does the scale need on the left to be balanced?

   a. 250 g   b. 100 g

   c. 500 g   d. 750 g

3. You have four 50 g weights, two 100 g weghts, and one 250 g weight. How can you balance the scale?

   TWo 100g + ones50g weghts = one 250g weights.

Name: _____ **Date:** _____

Directions: Read the text, and answer the questions.

Savannah is on a seesaw with her dad. When they are both sitting on the seesaw, she is up, and her dad is down.

1. How could Savannah's dad cause his side to go up?

   a. Use force to push it up.

   b. Use force to pull it down.

   c. Put his arms up.

   d. Do nothing.

2. If Savannah was on the seesaw with a friend who was the same weight, could they balance it?

   a. Yes, because both sides would have the same amount of force pushing down on them.

   b. No, you cannot balance a seesaw.

3. What question could you ask to find out more about how to make the seesaw work?

   _____

   _____

   _____

Name: _____ **Date:** _____

Directions: Read the text, and answer the questions.

John and his friends are preparing packages of cookies for a bake sale. They are using a pan balance to weigh the cookies. They want to put them in packages of equal weight.

1. To make sure that the packages are equal weights, John should _____ .

   a. include a different number of cookies in each package

   b. guess if they're the same weight

   c. put cookies in the pan balance until it is level

   d. hold the packages in his hand until they feel equal

2. When John uses the pan balance to weigh the packages, _____ .

   a. it should be level

   b. it should tilt to the left

   c. it should tilt to the right

   d. it will tell John the actual weight

3. How could John use the scale if he wanted to make some packages lighter?

   _____

   _____

Planning Solutions

Name: _____ Date: _____

Directions: Look at the pictures, and answer the questions.

1. Explain how the people are using force to move the seesaw.

   _____

   _____

   _____

   _____

2. What is the pattern you observe when a seesaw moves?

   _____

   _____

   _____

   _____

3. If neither person used force, what would happen?

   _____

   _____

   _____

Communicating Results

ABC

Name: _____ **Date:** _____

Directions: Read the text, and answer the questions.

Going Back and Forth

Swinging happens when you push or pull an object that is hanging. The object will move back and forth. Over time, the object swings less. Gravity will eventually stop the swing. Gravity is a downward force that pulls objects toward Earth.

1. Swinging occurs when _____ .

   a. an object bounces up and down

   b. a ball rolls down a hill

   c. two objects move in the exact same way

   d. a hanging object moves back and forth

2. A swing's motion will always be _____ .

   a. rough and bumpy

   b. back and forth

   c. round and round

   d. fast and slow

3. What happens over time to the distance that a swing travels?

   a. It gets further and further.

   b. It keeps going up.

   c. It gets shorter and shorter.

   d. It stops immediately.

Name: _____ **Date:** _____

Directions: When you swing, you go back and forth. If someone pulls you back, you swing forward about the same distance.

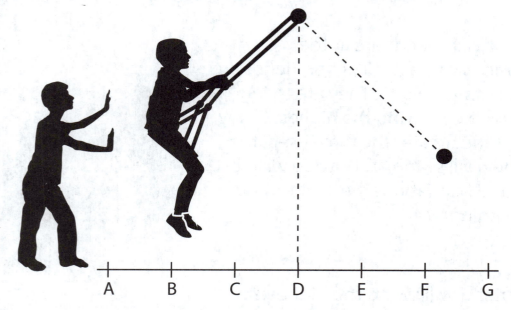

1. If someone pulls you back to B and lets go, where will you swing?

   a. C   **b.** D

   c. F   **d.** G

2. What happens if your friend pushes you hard and you swing to G?

   a. You will swing back to A.   **b.** You will swing back to B.

   c. You will stay at G.   **d.** You will stop at D.

3. What should you change to affect how far you swing?

   a. the direction of the force   **b.** the amount of force applied

   c. the color of the swing   **d.** the thickness of the chains

Developing Questions

Name: _____ Date: _____

Directions: Read the text, and answer the questions.

Kate and her friends are at the playground swinging. All of her friends are about the same weight. They are trying to guess who can swing the highest. They know that the greater the force used, the higher they will swing. The swing will go forward and back about the same amount when swinging.

1. Which friend will swing the highest?

   a. whoever is the tallest one

   b. whoever gets pushed with the greatest force

   c. whoever is on the lightest swing

   d. whoever is on the swing with the blue seat

2. If Kate's swing travels 8 feet forward, about how far will it travel backward?

   a. 0 feet

   b. 2 feet

   c. 8 feet

   d. 16 feet

3. What can you ask about force and swinging?

   does the Hrevest go the Highest?

   _____

   _____

Name: _____ **Date:** _____

Directions: Read the text, and answer the questions.

Raj and his friends are taking turns swinging on a tire swing. They want to go as fast as possible on the tire swing. They realize that a short chain makes the swing travel faster.

1. What should they do in order to swing faster on the tire swing?

   a. don't push the swing

   b. use a different color tire

   c. push with less force

   d. use a shorter length of chain

2. What does Raj need to go slow on the tire swing?

   a. short chains

   b. long chains

   c. a red tire

   d. a push with more force

3. How can Raj learn more about what affects the speed of the swing?

    Shrug.

   _____

   _____

Communicating Results

Name: _____ **Date:** _____

Directions: Read the text. Draw an arrow to show the direction of force from the squirrel. Draw another arrow to show which way the bird house will swing. Then, answer the question.

A squirrel jumps from a tree trunk and lands on a bird house that is hanging from one of the branches.

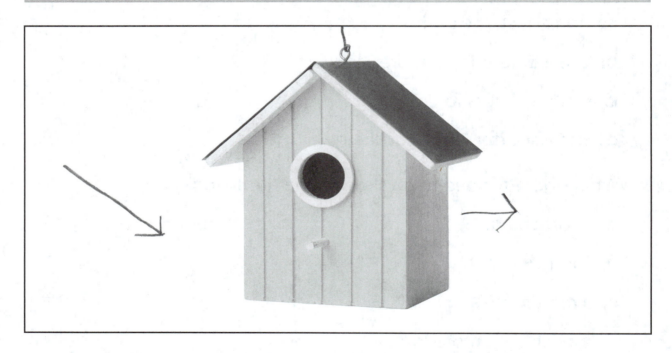

1. Explain how you figured out the direction that the bird house will swing.

_____

_____

_____

Name: _____ **Date:** _____

Directions: Read the text, and answer the questions.

Forces Going in Circles

Have you ever played with a spinning top? You use a turning force to spin the top. It moves in a circular motion while balancing on its tip. It spins in a circle because it follows the direction of the force applied. It will keep spinning until other forces cause it to slow down and stop.

1. What is needed to spin an object?

   a. a turning force

   b. a strong pulling force

   c. bouncing up and down

   d. pushing straight ahead

2. A spinning motion is _____ .

   a. back and forth

   b. up and down

   c. never the same

   d. circular

3. The motion of the object _____ the force.

   a. goes in the opposite direction of

   b. works against

   c. follows the direction of

   d. doesn't pay attention to

4. Tell a friend about different things you have spun using force.

Name: _____ Date: _____

Directions: Karen and her friends are at a playground. There is a merry-go-round there. The chart shows the force used to push the merry-go-round. Read it, and answer the questions.

Analyzing Data

Amount of Force in Push	Speed
low	slow
medium	medium
high	fast

1. How much force is needed to get the merry-go-round to spin slowly?

   a. high   b. medium

   c. low   d. no force is needed

2. When Karen pushes the merry-go-round, _____ .

   a. it moves in the direction of her push   b. it moves in the opposite direction of her push

   c. it slows down when she pushes with a lot of force   d. it goes faster when she pushes it with gentle force

3. Which tool could Karen use to measure how fast the merry-go-round is going?

   a. ruler   b. timer

   c. camera   d. magnifying glass

4. What other ways can Karen change the merry-go-round's motion?

   a. add weight   b. direction of push

   c. position of riders   d. all of the above

Name: _____ Date: _____

Directions: Read the text, and answer the questions.

> Dana wants to play her favorite game. The spinner for the game is not working the way that it should. The spinner is a circle of thick cardboard with a plastic arrow attached to the center. Dana can't get the arrow part of the spinner to spin.

1. If the spinner was working correctly, it would _____ .

   a. slow down when she spins it quickly

   b. spin quickly when she pushes it gently

   c. spin in the direction that she pushes it

   d. speed up when she spins it with less force

2. How does Dana know the spinner isn't working?

   a. The color of the spinner is different.

   b. The arrow doesn't move when force is applied to it.

   c. The cardboard is thick.

   d. The spinner is four inches long.

3. Dana wants to make her own spinner. What question can she ask to help guide her design?

   can I use same of the spinner?

   _____

   _____

Name: _____ **Date:** _____

Directions: Read the text, and answer the questions.

> Michael and his three friends are riding a merry-go-round at the playground. His dad is pushing it. When they stand on the edge and spin fast, they have to hold on tight so they don't fly off. When they all stand on the merry-go-round at the same time, it's harder to push.

1. What causes Michael and his friends to feel like they will fly off?

    a. The force of standing still.

    b. The force of the spin.

    c. The force of holding on.

    d. The force of their hands on the handles.

2. When everyone stands on the merry-go round, _____ .

    a. it will take more force to spin

    b. it will take less force to spin

    c. it will move in the opposite direction of the force

    d. it will move quickly with less force

3. What can Michael do to figure out what makes the merry-go-round easiest to push?

    _____

    _____

Name: _____ **Date:** _____

Directions: Read the text, and study the chart. Graph the results of Tom's experiment.

Tom built a marble track. He rolls the marble three separate times with different amounts of force. Each time, he records the time it takes the marble to go around the track once.

Amount of Force Used	Time
low	10 seconds
medium	8 seconds
high	5 seconds

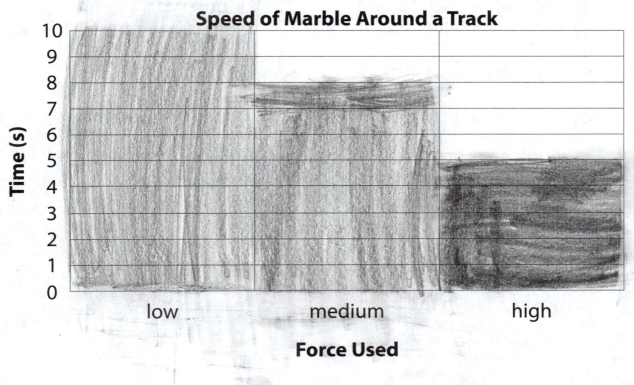

Speed of Marble Around a Track

Time (s)

low   medium   high

Force Used

Communicating Results

Learning Content

Name: BLYThe   **Date:** _____

Directions: Read the text, and answer the questions.

Hair-Raising Balloons

Rubbing two things together can charge the objects with static electricity. You can see this when socks stick together out of the dryer. You can also see it when you rub an inflated balloon on your hair. As you pull the balloon away slowly, the hair stands up. The hair and the balloon are pulled to each other. If the balloon is close, the pull is strong, and the hair stands very tall. If it is farther away, the pull is weaker.

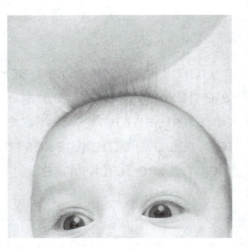

1. What is the effect of rubbing an inflated balloon on hair?

   a. The hair changes color.

   b. The hair falls out.

   c. The hair is charged with static electricity.

   d. More hair will grow in the spot rubbed by the balloon.

2. Holding a charged balloon close to charged hair _____.

   a. will have a strong pull

   b. will have a weak pull

   c. won't have any effect

   d. will pop the balloon

3. How do you need to hold the balloon to make the hair stand very tall?

   a. closer to the hair

   b. farther from the hair

   c. by the knot in the balloon

   d. with gloves on

Name: _____ **Date:** _____

Directions: This graph shows the relationship between rubs of a balloon and the amount of static electricity. Study the graph. Then, answer the questions.

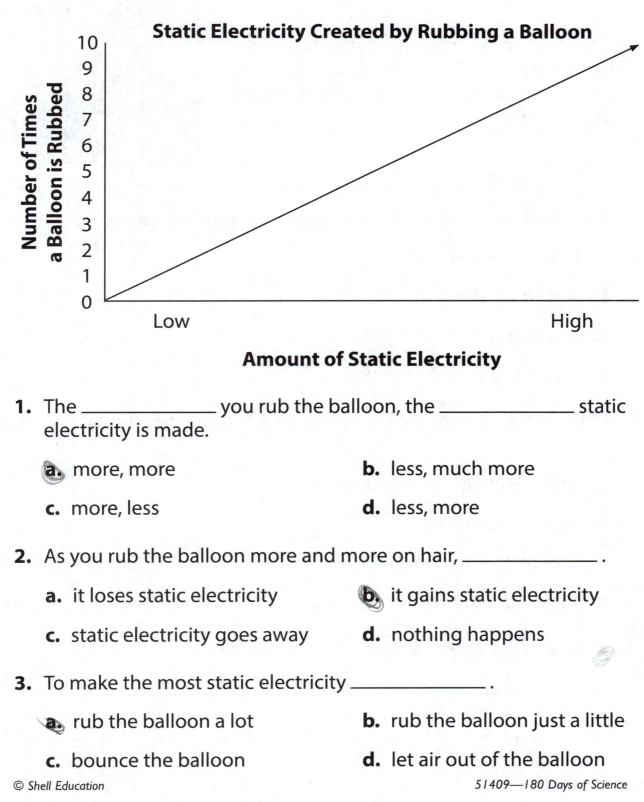

Static Electricity Created by Rubbing a Balloon

Number of Times a Balloon is Rubbed

Amount of Static Electricity

Analyzing Data

1. The _____ you rub the balloon, the _____ static electricity is made.

   a. more, more
   b. less, much more
   c. more, less
   d. less, more

2. As you rub the balloon more and more on hair, _____ .

   a. it loses static electricity
   b. it gains static electricity
   c. static electricity goes away
   d. nothing happens

3. To make the most static electricity _____ .

   a. rub the balloon a lot
   b. rub the balloon just a little
   c. bounce the balloon
   d. let air out of the balloon

Name: _____ **Date:** _____

Directions: Read the text, and answer the questions.

Students rub a balloon on wool to charge it with static electricity. Then they are able to stick it to the wall. Over time, it starts to slide down the wall.

1. What happens when a charged balloon is touched to a wall?

   a. It pops immediately.

   b. It sticks to the wall.

   c. It falls quickly to the ground.

   d. It starts to float up the wall.

2. If the students want the balloon to stick longer, they should _____ .

   a. use a different color balloon

   b. use a shiny balloon

   c. charge it with more static electricity

   d. make sure the balloon has less static electricity

3. Write a question about using static electricity.

   _____

   _____

Name: _____ Date: _____

Directions: Read the text, and answer the questions.

Students in a class are experimenting with static electricity. They rub a balloon on a piece of wool for five seconds. Then they stick it to the wall. It sticks to the wall for eight seconds. Then they rub the balloon on the wool for 10 seconds. This time, it sticks to the wall for 12 seconds.

1. What will happen if the students rub the balloon on the wool for longer than 10 seconds?

   a. It will stick to the wall for two seconds.

   b. It will stick to the wall for longer than 12 seconds.

   c. It will stick to the wall for eight seconds.

   d. It will not stick to the wall.

2. Why does rubbing the balloon on the wool for longer increase the time it sticks to the wall?

   a. It charges the balloon with more static electricity.

   b. It charges the balloon with less static electricity.

   c. It does not charge the balloon with static electricity.

   d. It makes the surface of the balloon sticky.

3. What could students change about the experiment to further test static electricity?

   _____

   _____

Communicating Results

Name: _____ **Date:** _____

Directions: Read the text. Draw two pictures of yourself. One should show you with a balloon making your hair stand up a lot. The other should show the balloon making your hair stand up less.

When you rub a balloon on your hair, it charges it with static electricity. The closer you hold it to your hair, the higher your hair will stand.

Name: _____ Date: _____

Directions: Read the text, and answer the questions.

They Are So Attractive!

A magnet is a rock or piece of metal that pushes or pulls certain types of metal. Magnets can be used to attract or repel other magnets. Attract means they are pulled together. Repel means they are pushed apart. They can also push or pull certain types of metal, like iron. The distance between objects will affect the force of the push or pull. The closer they are, the greater the force. The farther apart they are, the weaker the force.

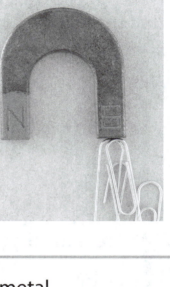

1. A magnet can _____ certain types of metal.

   a. become cold near

   b. bounce

   c. move around

   d. push or pull

2. What does the distance between magnetic objects determine?

   a. what color they are

   b. how fast they fall

   c. how strong they attract or repel

   d. how high they bounce

3. What will most likely create the greatest force between two magnets?

   a. putting them close together

   b. placing them far apart

   c. dropping them to the ground

   d. squeezing one tightly in your hand

Name: _____ Date: _____

Directions: Read the text, and study the pictures. Then, answer the questions.

Drew is using his magnet to pick up iron shavings. As he slides his magnet closer, he picks up more and more shavings. He knows that the heavier the iron is, the less the magnet will move it.

Plcture 1   Plcture 2   Plcture 3

1. Where is the magnetic attraction the strongest?

   a. Picture 1   **b.** Picture 2

   c. Picture 3   **d.** The attraction stays
                                      the same.

2. Where is the magnetic attraction the weakest?

   a. Picture 1   **b.** Picture 2

   c. Picture 3   **d.** The attraction stays
                                      the same.

3. Tom thinks that if he uses a heavy iron block instead of iron shavings, it will affect his experiment. Is he correct?

   a. Yes, the magnet won't move   **b.** No, the size of the objet
        the block as much.   doesn't matter.

   c. Yes, the magnet will move   **d.** No, magnets only work
        the block more.   with iron shavings, not
                                               iron blocks.

Analyzing Data

Name: _____ **Date:** _____

Directions: Read the text, and answer the questions.

A magnetic field is an area around a magnetic object. This is where you can observe a magnetic force. Earth has a magnetic field. This is because the center of Earth is metal. A compass is a tool that shows which direction you are facing—north, south, east, or west. It has a small magnet that is attracted to Earth's magnetic field. A compass always points north.

1. What principle does a compass use to tell direction?

    a. gravity

    b. speed

    c. magnetism

    d. electricity

2. A student thinks that if she spins around, the compass won't work anymore. Is she correct?

    a. Yes, the compass will always point straight ahead.

    b. No, the compass will always point north.

    c. Yes, the compass does not spin.

    d. No, the compass will always point south.

3. Write a question about how a compass shows direction.
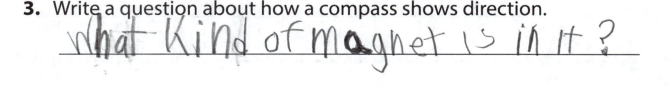
    What kind of magnet is in it?

    _____

    _____

Name: _____ **Date:** _____

Directions: Read the text, and answer the questions.

> Ella is studying an iron ring. The ring fell off the table and rolled behind a heavy bookcase. Ella wonders if she can use magnets to get it back. She knows iron is attracted to magnets.

Planning Solutions

1. What property would Ella be using to get the iron ring?

   a. gravity

   b. magnetism

   c. weight

   d. force

2. Will Ella be able to use magnets to get the iron ring?

   a. No, the magnets only work with other magnets.

   b. Yes, the magnets can move the bookcase.

   c. Yes, the magnets will attract the iron ring.

   d. No, the magnets will repel the iron ring further away.

3. Ella has a long magnet that will reach close to the ring. She also has a short magnet that won't reach as close. Which should she use, and why?

   _____

   _____

   _____

   _____

Name: _____ **Date:** _____

Directions: Study the chart. Complete the bar graph using the data in the chart. Then, answer the question.

Magnet	Number of Paper Clips Attracted
Magnet 1	3 paper clips
Magnet 2	8 paper clips
Magnet 3	5 paper clips
Magnet 4	11 paper clips

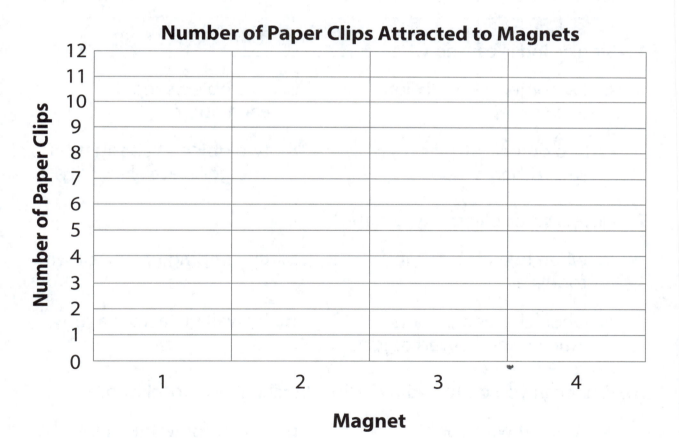

Number of Paper Clips Attracted to Magnets

1. Which magnet is the strongest? How can you tell?

_____

_____

Communicating Results

Name: _____ **Date:** _____

Directions: Read the text, and answer the questions.

A "Sticky" Situation

Zap! Have you ever touched a door knob and gotten a shock? Maybe you've rubbed blankets together in the dark and seen sparks. These zaps and sparks are the result of static electricity. It is created when two things rub against each other. The more you rub objects together, the more static electricity they create. They stay charged until they touch something that is not charged, like a door knob.

1. Static cling is caused when _____ .

   a. two objects bounce off each other

   b. two objects repel each other

   c. two objects attract each other

   d. two objects rub together and generate electricity

2. How is static electricity released?

   a. when two objects rub together

   b. by jumping up and down

   c. when charged objects touch non-charged objects

   d. by walking across a rug

3. What can you do to avoid getting shocked by a doorknob?

   a. Touch it with your other hand.

   b. Touch something else before the doorknob.

   c. Rub your feet on the carpet first.

   d. There is no way to avoid getting shocked.

Name: _____ **Date:** _____

Directions: Jake notices that whenever he walks on a rug then touches a doorknob, he gets shocked. The longer he walks on the rug, the greater the shock. Study the graph, and answer the questions.

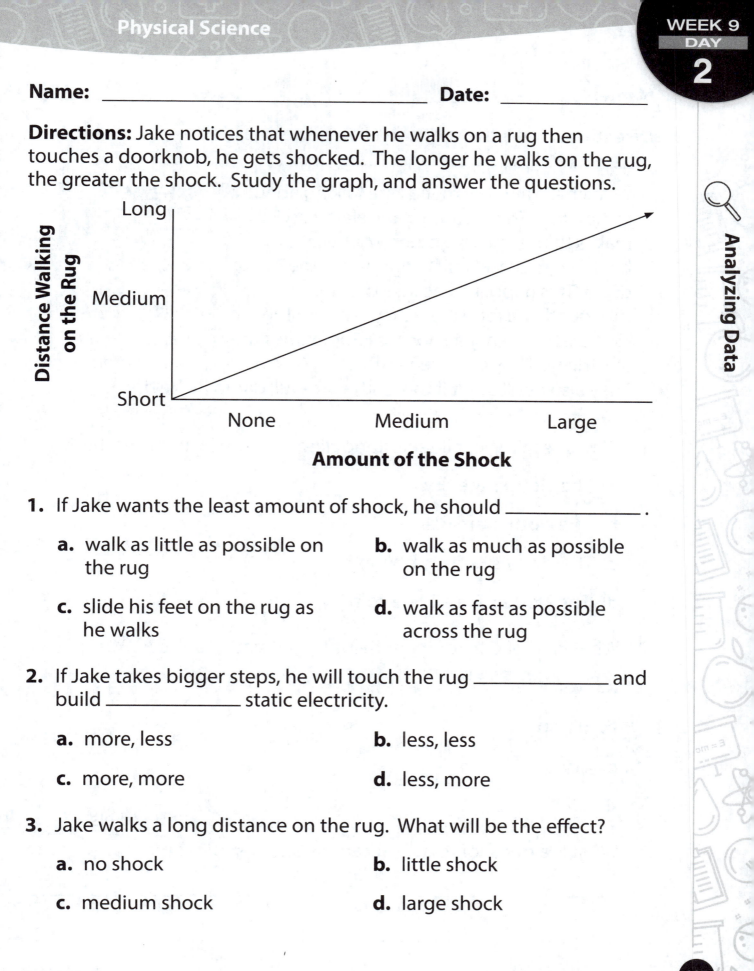

Amount of the Shock

Analyzing Data

1. If Jake wants the least amount of shock, he should _____.

   a. walk as little as possible on the rug

   b. walk as much as possible on the rug

   c. slide his feet on the rug as he walks

   d. walk as fast as possible across the rug

2. If Jake takes bigger steps, he will touch the rug _____ and build _____ static electricity.

   a. more, less

   b. less, less

   c. more, more

   d. less, more

3. Jake walks a long distance on the rug. What will be the effect?

   a. no shock

   b. little shock

   c. medium shock

   d. large shock

Name: _____ **Date:** _____

Directions: Read the text, and answer the questions.

> Michelle and her friends are talking about static cling. This is when static electricity makes things stick together. Michelle says her family's clothes stick together in the dryer. This happens because the clothes rub together a lot. When they take out the clothes, they can get shocked. Sometimes they can even see the electricity. They don't see static cling on clothes in the washer. They also don't see it if the clothes are still damp in the dryer.

1. Why doesn't Michelle see static cling on clothes in the washer?

   a. The clothes are dry.

   b. The clothes are wet.

   c. The clothes don't rub together.

   d. The clothes are all one color.

2. What kind of environment helps to generate static cling?

   a. wet

   b. damp

   c. dry

   d. cold

3. What is a question that you can ask about static cling?

   _____

   _____

Name: _____ **Date:** _____

Directions: Read the text. Then, answer the questions.

> Sarah and her friends are talking about static cling. She says clothes in the dryer sometimes stick together. One of the friends says her clothes don't stick together. Her family uses dryer sheets. She thought that the dryer sheets were to make the clothes smell nice. Now she realizes that the dryer sheets rubbing on the clothes also takes away the static cling.

Planning Solutions

1. Why might dryer sheets help reduce static cling?

   a. Their color helps absorb the static cling.

   b. They rub against all of the clothes and transfer the electricity.

   c. The smell of the sheets takes away the static cling.

   d. They help the dryer to dry the clothes.

2. How can the group of friends test if the dryer sheets reduce static cling?

   a. Run the dryer with clothes inside.

   b. Run the dryer without heat.

   c. Dry clothes with and without dryer sheets.

   d. Read the box of dryer sheets.

3. What do you think might happen if you rubbed a dryer sheet on clothes that were stuck together?

   _____

   _____

Name: _____ Date: _____

Directions: Read the text. Draw a diagram of before and after Robin rubs the wool on the rod. Label your diagrams, and answer the question.

ABC

Communicating Results

> Robin is studying static electricity. She uses a plastic rod and small pieces of paper. She puts the rod over the paper. Nothing happens. Then she rubs the plastic rod with a piece of wool fabric. When she holds the plastic rod over the pieces of paper, they fly up and cling to the rod.

Before	After

1. Explain your diagrams.

_____

_____

_____

Learning Content

Name: _____ **Date:** _____

Directions: Read the text, and answer the questions.

Super Magnets

Super magnets are a special type of magnet. They are very strong. This means they can be small and still have a strong force. Many products use magnets. Appliances, electronics, and speakers all use them. Super magnets work well in these products because they are small, strong, and lightweight.

1. What is significant about super magnets?

   a. They are larger with the same amount of strength.

   b. They can be made into any shape.

   c. They are much stronger than regular magnets.

   d. They have reversed polarity.

2. When would someone use super magnets?

   a. when a very small and strong magnet is needed

   b. when a magnet is needed to stick to wood

   c. when a regular magnet is too strong for a project

   d. when a magnet is needed to be in a special shape

3. Which is an example of a good use of super magnets?

   a. cleaning up iron shavings

   b. holding a piece of paper on a filing cabinet

   c. a hook to hold a paper calendar

   d. holding a refrigerator door shut

Analyzing Data

Name: _____ Date: _____

Directions: The strength of some super magnets vary by temperature Study the chart. Then, answer the questions.

Magnet Type	Ideal Temperature
1	very cold
2	room temperature
3	very hot

1. Which type of magnet would you use if you were working in the South Pole?

   a. 1   **b.** 2

   c. 3   **d.** any of them

2. What do you think happens when you bring a type 1 magnet to a very hot environment?

   a. It gets stronger.   **b.** It gets weaker.

   c. It changes color.   **d.** Nothing happens.

3. What conclusion can you draw from the table?

   a. Super magnets are strongest at specific temperatures.   **b.** You should carefully choose what magnet to use based on the environment.

   c. Not all magnets are the best for all situations.   **d.** all of the above

4. Which type of magnet would be best to use in your home? Why?

   _____

   _____

Name: _____ **Date:** _____

Directions: Read the text, and answer the questions.

Cleaning the algae off of the inside of fish tanks is made easier by super magnets. The tank can be cleaned without having to reach your arm into the tank. The strong magnets hold the brush on the inside of the tank to the handle on the outside of the tank.

1. How do the magnets help the cleaning tool clean the tank?

    a. The algae are attracted to the magnets.

    b. The magnets repel the algae away from the glass.

    c. They hold the brush to the handle on the oustide of the tank.

    d. The cleaner stirs up the water to rinse off the side of the tank.

2. Which question would help you decide if two magnets would work in a tank cleaner?

    a. Are the magnets lightweight?

    b. Will the magnets work through glass?

    c. How do the magnets work when warm?

    d. Can the magnets be used on refrigerators?

3. Write a question that can help you find out more about how the magnets help clean the tank.

    _____

    _____

Name: _____ **Date:** _____

Directions: Read the text, and answer the questions.

> George has liquids he needs to stir. He wants to use a magnetic stirrer. It has a magnetic bar that he puts in the liquid. The beaker sits on a stirring device. When he turns it on, magnets in the device rotate and cause the magnetic bar to also rotate.

1. For the magnetic stirrer to work, the magnets _____ .

   a. need to directly touch

   b. need to rotate

   c. need to be weak

   d. need to be a certain temperature

2. Which would be an advantage of using magnetic stirrers?

   a. They can only stir liquids slowly.

   b. The liquids must be at a certain temperature.

   c. The liquids are not mixed as well.

   d. They can stir liquids for long periods of time.

3. What could George do to find out more about how the magnetic stirrer works?

   _____

   _____

Name: _____ **Date:** _____

Directions: Read the text. Then, follow the steps.

> James takes two toy cars and tapes a bar magnet on top of each. Each magnet has a north pole (n) and a south pole (s). He knows that opposite poles attract and that like poles repel. Repel means to push away.

1. Label the diagram to show how James should place the magnets so that the cars will move away from each other.

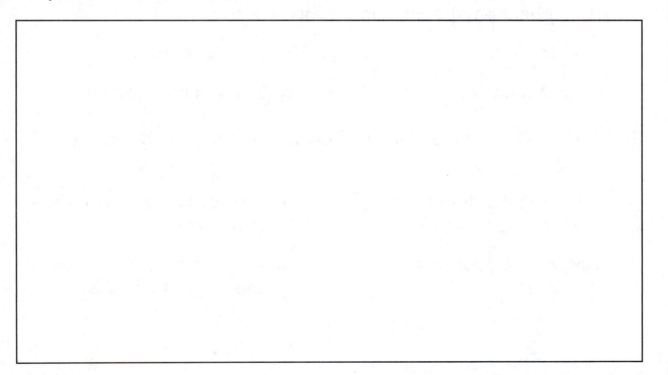

2. Draw and label a diagram to show how the magnets should be placed so that the cars will move toward each other.

Communicating Results

Learning Content

Name: _____ **Date:** _____

Directions: Read the text, and answer the questions.

Keeping Things Closed

Magnets can be used in many ways. You can have fun playing with them. They can also be used for specific tasks. You can use magnets when things need to be joined or separated. Magnets can be used to keep purses or jewelry clasps closed. They can be used to keep cabinet doors closed, too.

1. Magnets are a great choice for items that _____ .

   a. need to bounce up and down

   b. need to stop and start

   c. need to attract and release

   d. need to change color

2. What other items could magnets be used for?

   a. a bicycle tire

   b. a refrigerator door

   c. a water faucet

   d. a children's wagon

3. What could be done to lessen how tightly a cabinet door stays closed?

   a. Loosen the door hinges a lot.

   b. Change the door color to a light color.

   c. Make the door twice as large.

   d. Increase the space between the magnetic clasps.

Name: _____ **Date:** _____

Directions: Different kinds of clasps are made to have different kinds of holding power. Study the chart, and answer the questions.

Clasp	Ease of Opening	Attraction Strength (1—easiest, 4—strongest)
clasp 1	very easy	1 (good for cabinet doors)
clasp 2	easy	2 (good for jewelry)
clasp 3	medium	3 (good for holding knives against a wall)
clasp 4	difficult	4 (good for appliances)

1. What type of magnetic clasp would be best for expensive jewelry?

   a. 1

   b. 2

   c. 3

   d. 4

2. Clasp 1 would be best _____ .

   a. on a kitchen cabinet door

   b. holding a glass picture frame on the wall

   c. to hold sharp knives against a wall

   d. holding expensive sunglasses to their frame

3. Bob is a bus driver. He wants to install a cabinet inside of his bus to hold his tools. What type of magnet would work best on the cabinet door?

   a. 1

   b. 2

   c. 3

   d. 4

Developing Questions

Name: _____ **Date:** _____

Directions: Read the text, and answer the questions.

> Today's refrigerators work differently than old ones. They used to have latches that opened and closed the door. Now they have magnets in the door. The force between the magnets is the strongest when the door is closed. It is weakest when the door is open all the way.

1. When is the force between the magnets in the doors the greatest?

   a. When they are open all the way.

   b. When they are open a small amount.

   c. When they are closed halfway.

   d. When they are closed all the way.

2. If a refrigerator door closes but pops open, what does this mean?

   a. The door may need more magnets.

   b. The magnets may be too strong.

   c. There may be too many magnets.

   d. The magnets might have a strong attraction.

3. Write a question that you have about magnets in a refrigerator door.

   _____

   _____

Name: _____ **Date:** _____

Directions: Read the text, and answer the questions.

Magnets can be used in many ways. They can be used to keep things closed. You are designing a folder with a magnetic closure. It needs to stay closed without popping open.

1. In your first design, the folder tears when you open it. Which of the following could help?

    a. adding more magnets to the closure

    b. using fewer magnets in the closure

    c. using thinner paper for the folder

    d. using stronger magnets

2. How would using thicker paper for the folder affect the design?

    a. It would increase the distance between the magnets.

    b. It would decrease the distance between the magnets.

    c. It would increase the attraction between the magnets.

    d. It would decrease the repelling force between the magnets.

3. How else could you improve the design of the folder?

    _____

    _____

    _____

Communicating Results

Name: _____ **Date:** _____

Directions: Read the text. Complete the chart based on the information in the text. Then, answer the question.

An engineer is creating a magnetic closure for a box flap. He is using two magnets. One is on the box. The other is on the flap. First he puts the magnets five inches apart. The flap closes, but the magnets do not hold it closed. Then he puts one magnet lower than the other. The flap closes, but is easy to open. When the magnets are placed directly across from each other, they click together, and the flap stays closed.

Magnet Position	Observations	Example
Directly across from each other		
One lower than the other		
5 inches apart		

1. Which position of the magnets works best for the box closure?

_____

Name: _____ **Date:** _____

Directions: Read the text, and answer the questions.

Magnetic Clean-Up Crew

Magnets are attracted to other magnets. They are also attracted to certain metals like iron and steel. They are not attracted to plastic, wood, or glass. This means that magnets can be used to separate some metals from other things. They can be used in construction site cleanup. They can also be used to sort materials for recycling.

1. Magnets are not attracted to _____ .

   a. iron

   b. wood

   c. steel

   d. other magnets

2. How can magnets make cleaning up easier?

   a. Magnets can pick up heavy wood.

   b. Cleaning up is impossible without magnets.

   c. Magnets can separate different types of materials.

   d. Magnets can pick up pieces of broken glass.

3. Can a magnet be used to pull iron shavings out of wood shavings?

   a. Yes, because magnets are attracted to iron.

   b. No, because magnets are not attracted to iron.

   c. Yes, because magnets are attracted to wood.

   d. No, because the magnets are attracted to iron and wood.

Analyzing Data

Name: _____ **Date:** _____

Directions: Different materials are attracted to magnets. Study the chart. Then, answer the questions.

Material	Attracted to Magnets?
glass	no
plastic	no
iron	yes
rubber	no
steel	yes
wood	no
aluminum	no

1. What are three items that are not attracted to magnets?

   a. iron, glass, rubber

   b. iron, steel, aluminum

   c. plastic, steel, aluminum

   d. plastic, aluminum, glass

2. If you have a pile of glass, plastic, and aluminum, can you use a magnet to separate them?

   a. Yes, because magnets can separate different types of materials.

   b. No, because magnets aren't attracted to any of these.

   c. Yes, because magnets are attracted to only aluminum.

   d. No, because magnets are attracted to each of these.

3. Will magnets separate iron and steel? Why or why not?

   _____

   _____

Name: _____ **Date:** _____

Directions: Read the text, and answer the questions.

John runs a junkyard. Here, old cars are taken apart. The parts are sorted with an electromagnet. This is a very strong magnet. It runs on electricity. It is much stronger than a regular magnet. John uses it to move very heavy pieces of metal.

1. What is the purpose of the electromagnet?

   a. to separate the metal from other materials in the cars

   b. to crush the car so parts can be separated

   c. to break the car into separate parts

   d. to recycle the metal

2. Why does John use an electromagnet instead of a regular magnet?

   a. The junkyard runs on electricity.

   b. Other magnets attract different materials.

   c. An electromagnet attracts glass and plastic as well as metal.

   d. It is stronger and can pick up heavier pieces of metal.

3. Using and electromagnet, John can also control the amount of magnetic force. What question could he ask to find out how he can use this?

   _____

   _____

Planning Solutions

Name: _____ **Date:** _____

Directions: Read the text, and answer the questions.

> Maddox and his friends are fishing in the local pond. Maddox uses steel fishing lures. Unfortunately, he accidentally drops one of his lures into the pond. In his tackle box, Maddox has a few magnets. He thinks that maybe he can use the magnets to get the lure back.

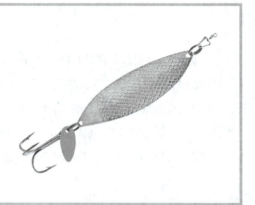

1. Will the magnets be helpful to Maddox?

    a. No, the magnets are only useful in the classroom.

    b. Yes, the magnets are attracted to the steel in the lures.

    c. No, the magnets don't help with catching fish.

    d. Yes, the magnets will attract fish.

2. If Maddox uses plastic fishing lures, will the magnets help him get them back?

    a. No, the plastic would be too heavy for the magnets.

    b. Yes, the magnets would attract the plastic.

    c. No, the plastic would not be attracted to the magnets.

    d. Yes, the plastic would be thin enough to be attracted by the magnets.

3. How can Maddox use the magnets to get his fishing lure back?

    _____

    _____

Name: _____ **Date:** _____

Directions: Draw and label magnetic objects near the circles. Then, label the rings either "strong pull" or "weak pull" to show how the objects will be affected by their distance from the magnet.

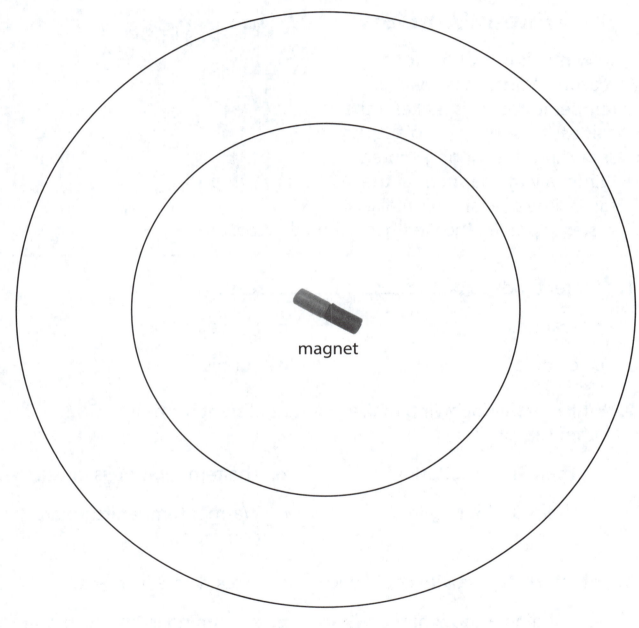

magnet

1. Explain why you placed the labels where you did.

_____

_____

Communicating Results

ABC

Earth and Space Science

Learning Content

Name: _____ **Date:** _____

Directions: Look at the picture, and read the text. Answer the questions.

Winter Wonders

Winter is one of our four seasons. Winter has lower temperatures. This makes it the coldest season. Some places have snow and sleet during winter. Winter always happens at the same time of year. This makes it easier to predict the weather during this season.

---

1. Winter tends to be the _____ season.

   a. warmest   **b.** rainiest

   c. coldest   **d.** sunniest

2. Which of the following makes winter different from the other seasons?

   a. There is precipitation.   **b.** The temperature is lower.

   c. There is a lot of rain.   **d.** Warmer temperatures are common.

3. Which winter activity could you do in places where it snows?

   a. building a snowman   **b.** swimming in an outdoor pool

   c. splashing around in puddles   **d.** playing soccer on a grassy field

Name: _____ **Date:** _____

Directions: The graph shows the temperatures recorded by a thermometer for an area in December. Study the graph, and answer the questions.

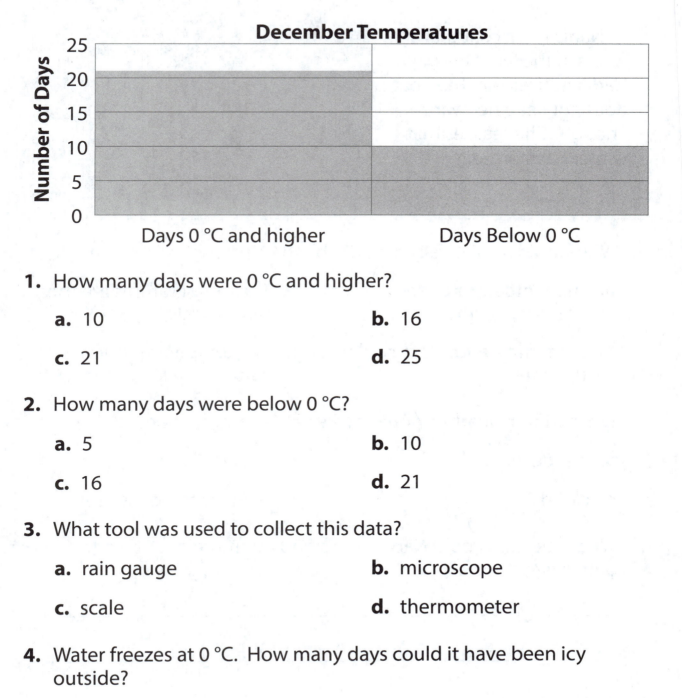

December Temperatures

1. How many days were 0 °C and higher?

    a. 10   **b.** 16

    c. 21   **d.** 25

2. How many days were below 0 °C?

    a. 5   **b.** 10

    c. 16   **d.** 21

3. What tool was used to collect this data?

    a. rain gauge   **b.** microscope

    c. scale   **d.** thermometer

4. Water freezes at 0 °C. How many days could it have been icy outside?

    _____

Analyzing Data

Name: _____ **Date:** _____

Directions: Read the text, and answer the questions.

Developing Questions

> Nadia has a coat that she wears in the fall. One day Nadia notices that this coat does not keep her warm enough. She realizes that winter has started.

1. Why would Nadia's fall coat NOT be the best choice in winter?

   a. The temperatures are warmer in winter.

   b. The temperatures are the same in fall.

   c. The temperatures are colder in winter.

   d. The temperatures are colder in fall.

2. What winter weather would make winter boots a good choice?

   a. gentle wind

   b. snow

   c. clouds

   d. warmer temperatures

3. What question could Nadia ask to find out more about winter patterns?

   _____

   _____

   _____

Name: _____ **Date:** _____

Directions: Kevin records the temperature and weather at the same time each day in January. Study his chart, and answer the questions.

Day	Temperature	Weather
Monday	28 °F	cloudy
Tuesday	27 °F	snowy
Wednesday	26 °F	snowy
Thursday	13 °F	cloudy

1. According to the chart, how many days were snowy?

   a. 1   **b.** 2

   c. 3   **d.** 4

2. What pattern did the temperature follow over these days?

   a. It decreased.   **b.** It increased.

   c. It stayed the same.   **d.** There is no pattern.

3. What can Kevin do to find out more about winter weather patterns?

   He can ask a _____

   _____

   _____

   _____

Name: _____ **Date:** _____

Directions: Read the information. Make a graph showing how many days had each type of weather. Then, answer the question.

| snowy days—8 | cloudy days—14 | sunny days—9 |

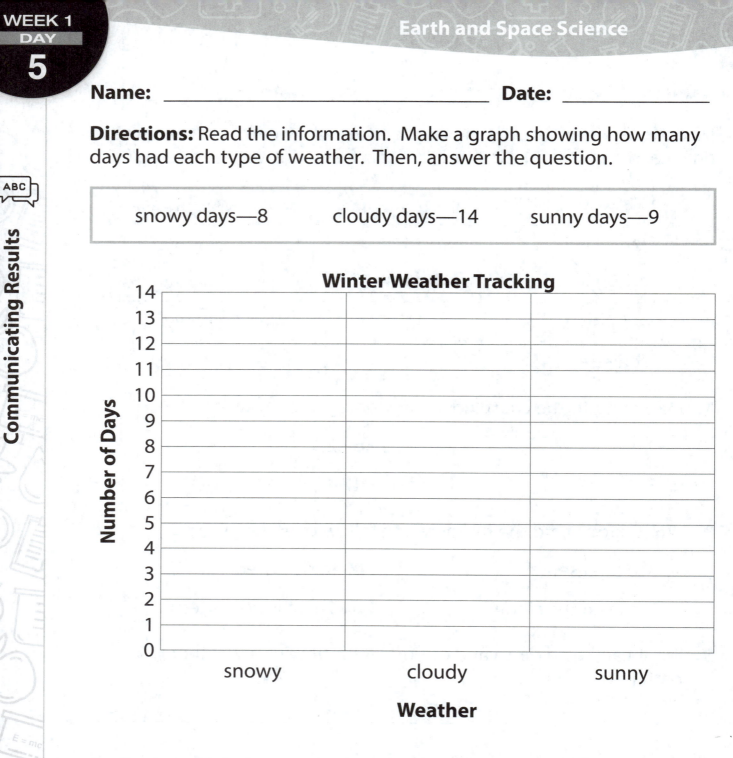

Winter Weather Tracking

Number of Days

snowy   cloudy   sunny

Weather

Communicating Results

1. Do you think the temperature was warmer during the snowy days or sunny days? Why?

   _____

   _____

   _____

Name: BLYTHE   **Date:** 5/10

Directions: Read the text, and answer the questions.

Spring Surprises

In spring, it starts to get warmer. The days become longer, so there is more daylight each day. New plants, flowers, and baby animals are all part of spring. Trees have buds for new leaves. Spring is warmer than winter, but not as warm as summer. Many places have rainstorms during this season as well.

1. Which pattern tells that it's spring?

   a. The temperature gets colder.

   b. The days get longer.

   c. The amount of rain decreases.

   d. The leaves fall from the trees.

2. What could you measure to see if spring is coming?

   a. the direction of the wind

   b. the number of leaves on the ground

   c. the number of clouds in the sky

   d. temperatures to see if they are getting warmer

3. When it is spring, trees _____ .

   a. are bare

   b. are full of green leaves

   c. have buds for new leaves

   d. have leaves changing color and falling

Analyzing Data

Name: _____ **Date:** _____

Directions: Spring begins in March and ends in June. The graph shows average high temperatures for the town where Milo lives. Study the chart, and answer the questions.

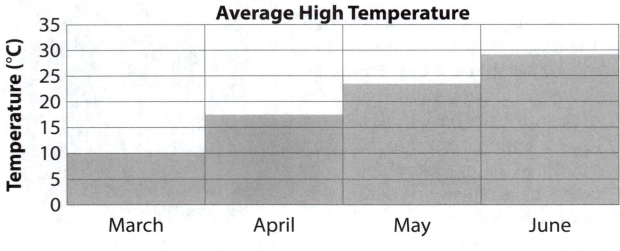

Average High Temperature

1. What is happening to the temperatures throughout spring?

   a. They are falling. **b.** They are rising.

   c. They rise, then fall. **d.** They fall, then rise.

2. Why are the average temperatures in March so much lower?

   a. Temperatures are rising from winter.

   b. Temperatures are rising from summer.

   c. Temperatures are falling from summer.

   d. Temperatures are falling from winter.

3. Based on the graph, what do you predict the temperatures would be like in July? Why?

   _____

   _____

Name: _____ **Date:** _____

Directions: Read the text, and answer the questions.

> Not all animals stay around when the weather becomes colder. They have other ways to survive the cold. As the spring weather warms, the animals begin to return.

Method	Definition	Animal Example
migration	Animals move from one region to another to find food and warmer weather.	Canada goose
hibernation	Animals go into a deep sleep to conserve energy during winter when food is scarce.	bears

1. What animals migrate?

   a. animals that have enough food

   b. animals that like the cold

   c. animals that need to find food

   d. animals that have shelter in the winter

2. Why would animals hibernate?

   a. to save energy when food is scarce

   b. because there is lots of food

   c. because it is very warm outside

   d. to find food in a warmer area

3. Write a question to help find out more about migration.

   _____

   _____

Developing Questions

Planning Solutions

Name: _____ **Date:** _____

Directions: Read the text, and answer the questions.

> Ava loves spring. She knows that it is when people plant gardens. She wants to know when she should plant tomatoes. They need a certain amount of sun and rain. There needs to be a pattern of warmer temperatures for a month before planting.

1. How long should Ava record the temperatures before planting?

   a. one hour

   b. one day

   c. one week

   d. one month

2. Which information would NOT be helpful for planning her garden?

   a. amount of sunlight

   b. temperature

   c. direction of wind

   d. amount of rain

3. What should Ava do next once she has the information that she needs for her garden?

   _____

   _____

   _____

   _____

Name: _____ **Date:** _____

Directions: Read the text, and look at the pictures. Use the pictures to write a weather prediction that makes the most sense on each blank line.

Weather predictions can be made by trying to follow a pattern of the weather. Below are two types of weather to use in the weather prediction.

partly cloudy

rainy

sunny _____

cloudy _____

rainy

1. Explain why you placed the predictions where you did.

   _____

   _____

   _____

2. What would be a reasonable prediction for the day after the last rainy day? Why?

   _____

   _____

Name: _____ **Date:** _____

Directions: Read the text, and answer the questions.

Summer Specials

Before we know it, spring becomes summer. Summer brings much warmer temperatures and long days. In many places, there is rain during the summer. Plants are growing, and trees are full of green leaves. Young animals born in the spring are growing up. When it gets very hot, people and animals look for relief from the heat and the sun.

1. Summer comes right after _____ .

   a. winter   **b.** spring

   c. a blizzard   **d.** fall

2. What happens when the temperatures rise?

   a. Days become shorter.   **b.** Plants grow more quickly.

   c. Animals look for shade.   **d.** There are more storms.

3. Which of the following tell you it's summer?

   a. a windy day during a week   **b.** the amount of rain in one month

   c. the number of sunny days during the year   **d.** the high temperatures

Name: _____ **Date:** _____

Directions: Bella is watching the weather. Study the weather forecast, and answer the questions.

1. What should Bella do to be prepared for the weather on Saturday?

   a. Bring an umbrella.

   b. Wear sunglasses.

   c. Wear a warm coat.

   d. Bring winter boots.

2. Bella looks at the map and predicts the weather for Tuesday to be _____.

   a. snowy

   b. rainy

   c. sunny

   d. windy

3. Which day will have the coolest temperatures?

   a. Saturday

   b. Sunday

   c. Wednesday

   d. Thursday

Name: _____ **Date:** _____

Directions: Read the text, and answer the questions.

Luis knows each season has its own weather patterns. Temperatures change. The amount of rain and snow changes. Rain can be measured with a rain gauge. Even wind directions can change. A wind sock can tell you its direction. He thinks about how summer is different.

1. Why aren't there blizzards in summer?

   a. The temperatures are too high.

   b. There is too much wind.

   c. There is not enough rain.

   d. There is not enough daylight.

2. What tool is used to measure summer precipitation?

   a. ruler

   b. wind sock

   c. rain gauge

   d. camera

3. What is a question that Luis can ask to learn more about summer weather patterns?

   _____

   _____

   _____

Name: _____ **Date:** _____

Directions: Read the text, and answer the questions.

Some seasons are hot. Some are cold. Temperatures were measured over long periods of time to show this pattern.

1. For summer, what would you predict the temperature to be?

   a. hot

   b. warm

   c. chilly

   d. freezing

2. How should temperature data be organized to show seasonal weather patterns?

   a. listed in order from highest to lowest

   b. written out in a paragraph

   c. Venn diagram

   d. bar graph

3. How could you find out if there is a temperature difference in the sun and in the shade?

   _____

   _____

   _____

Name: _____ **Date:** _____

Directions: Seasons follow patterns of weather. Circle the summer activities. Then, answer the questions.

outdoor hockey

swimming

building sandcastles

picking pumpkins

building a snowman

riding a bike

1. Explain why summer is a good time for the activities that you circled.

_____

_____

_____

_____

Name: _____ **Date:** _____

Directions: Read the text, and answer the questions.

Learning Content

Fall Features

The hot temperatures of summer begin to cool, and then fall begins. The days are shorter. The leaves on the trees start to change to brilliant colors—red, orange, and yellow. Then the leaves fall off of the trees as it gets closer to winter. The temperatures are cooler. Frost may form on the grass. These patterns of changes are how we know that fall is here.

1. In fall, _____ .

   a. temperatures are warmer

   b. leaves change color

   c. days are longer

   d. plants start to grow

2. Why does frost appear on the grass?

   a. because the ground is covered with leaves

   b. because there is a less sunlight

   c. because the air temperature is cooler

   d. because animals are storing food for winter

3. What can be measured to see if it is fall?

   a. the number of hours of daylight

   b. an increase in temperature

   c. the inches of snowfall

   d. the direction of the wind

Analyzing Data

Name: _____ **Date:** _____

Directions: The graph shows the average high and low temperatures for summer and fall in one town. Study the graph, and answer the questions.

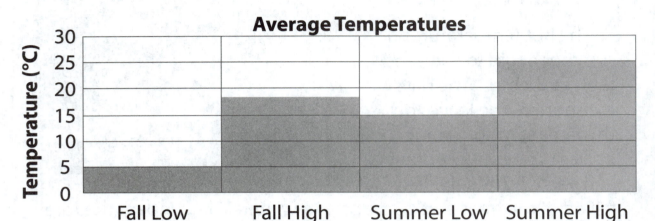

1. How do the low temperatures compare to each other?

   a. Fall is higher.   **b.** Summer is lower.

   c. Fall is lower.   **d.** The lows are the same.

2. What is the average high temperature in summer?

   a. 5 °C   **b.** 18 °C

   c. 15 °C   **d.** 25 °C

3. What pattern do you see?

   a. The fall high is higher than the summer high.

   b. The summer high is higher than the fall low.

   c. The fall low is higher than the summer low.

   d. The summer low is higher than the fall high.

Name: _____ **Date:** _____

Directions: Read the text, and look at the chart. Answer the questions.

> Tools are used to measure weather. The measurements help people observe patterns for each season.

Tool	What It Does
thermometer	measures air temperature
wind sock	shows the direction the wind is blowing
rain gauge	measures the amount of rain that falls
anemometer	measures the wind speed

1. Which tool would you use to find the direction of the wind?

   a. thermometer   **b.** wind sock

   c. rain gauge   **d.** anemometer

2. What are you measuring if you are using an anemometer?

   a. temperature   **b.** wind direction

   c. amount of rain   **d.** wind speed

3. Write a question that a thermometer could help you answer.

   _____

   _____

   _____

Developing Questions

Name: _____ **Date:** _____

Directions: Read the text, and answer the questions.

Earth moves around the sun. Earth is also tilted. This means that as it moves around the sun, different parts of Earth are tilted toward to the sun. The areas tilted toward the sun have summer. The areas tilted away from the sun have winter.

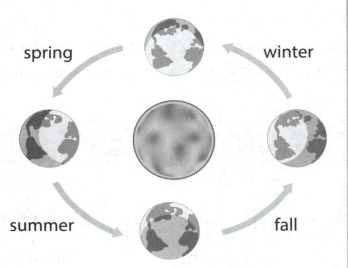

spring   winter

summer   fall

1. Summer occurs in an area when it is _____ .

   a. tilted toward the sun

   b. moving to tilt toward the sun

   c. tilted away from the sun

   d. moving to tilt away from the sun

2. Why does the area tilted away from the sun have winter?

   a. That area of Earth gets the most heat from the sun.

   b. That area receives the most hours of sun each day.

   c. That area of Earth gets the least heat from the sun.

   d. That area receives no sunlight.

3. What is the next step you can take to find out more about what causes fall's weather patterns?

   _____

   _____

Planning Solutions

Name: _____ **Date:** _____

Directions: Complete the diagram by writing a description for each season.

Fall	

Winter	

Spring	

Summer	

1. How do patterns help you write a description of each season?

_____

_____

_____

Learning Content

Name: _____ Date: _____

Directions: Read the text, and answer the questions.

Hot and Dry Lands

Different places in the world have different climates. Climate is the kind of weather an area has over very long periods of time.

Many deserts have a hot, dry climate. This does not mean that it is always hot and dry in the desert. It means that it is hot and dry in the desert most of the time.

1. What is the main characteristic of deserts?

   a. cold temperatures

   b. gentle breezes

   c. very little rain

   d. lots of shade

2. Deserts are so dry because of _____ .

   a. lots of wind

   b. cooler temperatures

   c. the sand

   d. low amounts of rain

3. Deserts _____ .

   a. are found where temperatures are hotter

   b. have frequent rain storms

   c. have lots of areas for shade

   d. are found where temperatures are cooler

Name: _____ **Date:** _____

Directions: Read the text, and study the chart. Then, answer the questions.

> Deserts are known for being hot and dry. Temperatures actually drop at night. The chart shows a desert's temperatures on one day. It also shows the rainfall the desert got in one year.

Desert Information	
temperature (during the day)	40 °C
temperature (at night)	-5 °C
annual rainfall	230 millimeters

1. During the day, _____ .

   a. the temperature is the lowest

   b. it is dark in the desert

   c. the temperature is at its highest

   d. it is difficult to measure the heat

2. What happens to the temperature as it goes from day to night?

   a. It decreases.

   b. It increases.

   c. It stays the same.

   d. It goes up and down.

3. The temperature of the desert _____ .

   a. is always changing

   b. mostly stays the same

   c. never changes

   d. gets the most rainfall

Developing Questions

Name: _____ **Date:** _____

Directions: Read the text, and answer the questions.

In hot and dry climates, it is hard for animals to be active during the day. It is too hot, so they find shelter instead. They come out at night when it is cooler.

1. Why do animals find shelter during the day?

   a. to avoid the heat

   b. to find water

   c. to dig burrows

   d. to hunt for food

2. Why do animals come out at night?

   a. There is more water available.

   b. They don't need to hide from predators.

   c. The temperatures are cooler.

   d. The temperatures have started to warm up.

3. Write a question that would help you learn more about how animals survive in hot and dry climates.

   _____

   _____

   _____

Name: _____ **Date:** _____

Directions: Read the text, and answer the questions.

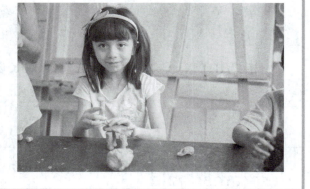

Alex wants to make a model of a desert to study the climate.

1. What is a reliable source of information for Alex to use?

   a. a fiction book   **b.** an encyclopedia

   c. an unknown website   **d.** a comic book

2. What is a characteristic of the desert that Alex should include in her model?

   a. lots of plants   **b.** cooler temperatures

   c. lots of rain   **d.** hot temperatures

3. What should Alex do once she has her model set up?

   _____

   _____

   _____

4. What other characteristics of a desert should Alex include?

   _____

   _____

Name: _____ **Date:** _____

Directions: Kareem is studying different types of desert plants. Read his chart, and answer the questions.

Plant	How It Survives in the Desert
elephant tree	Its thick trunk and lower limbs store water.
Ocotillo	It goes dormant during dry periods, and it grows during periods of rain.
desert marigold	Their hairy leaves increase the reflection of light and lower the leaf temperature.
saguaro cactus	They store most of the water they collect. They have a waxy coating that helps prevent water loss.

1. Which plants store water? Why is this useful for survival in the desert?

   _____

   _____

   _____

2. When a plant is dormant, it is alive but not actively growing. Why might the Ocotillo go dormant when there is no water available?

   _____

   _____

   _____

3. Which plant also uses spines to protect itself?

   _____

Name: _____ **Date:** _____

Directions: Read the text, and answer the questions.

It's a Jungle Out There

Rainforests are unique. The climate in a rainforest is warm all year. There is plenty of rain almost all year long. There tends to be less rain during the summer compared to the rest of the year. This warm and wet climate has many different kinds of plants and animals. The warm climate means that there is plenty of sun for all of the plants to grow.

1. What makes rainforests a good place for plants?

   a. cooler temperatures in summer

   b. lots of sunlight

   c. plenty of animals

   d. low amounts of rain

2. Rainforests are _____ .

   a. warm all year

   b. cooler in the summer

   c. dry during the winter

   d. dry all year

3. What would you observe if you visited a rainforest?

   a. plants that need to survive in a dry climate

   b. lots of plants and not many animals

   c. frequent snowfall

   d. frequent rainfall

Analyzing Data

Name: _____ **Date:** _____

Directions: Plants grow well in the rainforest climate. The way the plants grow creates different layers of plants in the rainforest. Study the chart. Then, answer the questions.

	Canopy	Forest Floor
Location	high off the ground	low and close to the ground
Sun	lots of sunlight	not much sunlight
Animals	most animals live here	fewer animals live here
Plants	many different plants live here	have large leaves to capture as much sunlight as possible

1. More living things live in the canopy because _____.

   a. the plants have large leaves   **b.** there are fewer animals

   c. more sunlight reaches this area   **d.** this area is closer to the ground

2. Why do the plants on the forest floor have larger leaves?

   a. Not as much sunlight reaches this area.   **b.** More animals live here.

   c. They are closer to the sun.   **d.** To shade other plants.

3. Where would you likely find a plant with very small leaves?

   a. forest floor   **b.** canopy

   c. both places   **d.** neither place

Name: _____ **Date:** _____

Directions: Read the text, and answer the questions.

> There are different parts to a rainforest. Each part gets a different amount of light. A new insect is found that lives only in the canopy.

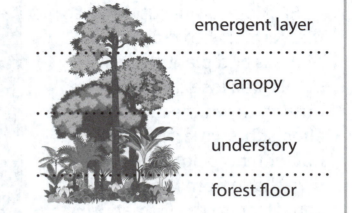

emergent layer

canopy

understory

forest floor

1. What might be the reason that this insect is not found in the emergent layer?

   a. There is not enough sunlight.

   b. Temperatures are too cold.

   c. The plant it needs is in the canopy.

   d. Its predator is not found there.

2. Why is the insect found only in the canopy?

   a. The canopy meets its specific needs.

   b. It needs shade from the sunlight.

   c. It eats dead leaves that fall to the ground.

   d. It needs to be as close to the sunlight as possible.

3. Write a question that would help you find out more about this insect.

   _____

   _____

   _____

Planning Solutions

Name: _____   Date: _____

Directions: Read the text, and answer the questions.

Rainforests are cut down so that farmers can plant crops. Animals and plants that live in this area lose their habitats. Cutting down the rainforest also affects the climate. The soil dries out with no plants and trees to give shade from the sun. This could lead to the formation of a desert.

1. Why are parts of the rainforests cut down?

   a. to keep the soil moist

   b. to make space to plant crops

   c. to decrease the amount of soil for planting

   d. to make room for more animals

2. Cutting down rainforests _____ .

   a. does not affect the climate

   b. makes the soil better

   c. affects the climate

   d. helps animals find homes

3. How could you learn more about saving the rainforests?

   _____

   _____

   _____

Name: _____ **Date:** _____

Directions: Read the text. Then use the text and pictures to complete the Venn diagram.

The Brazilian Tapir lives on the forest floor. The green iguana lives in the trees just below the canopy. Both of these animals live in the rainforest.

Tapir

Iguana

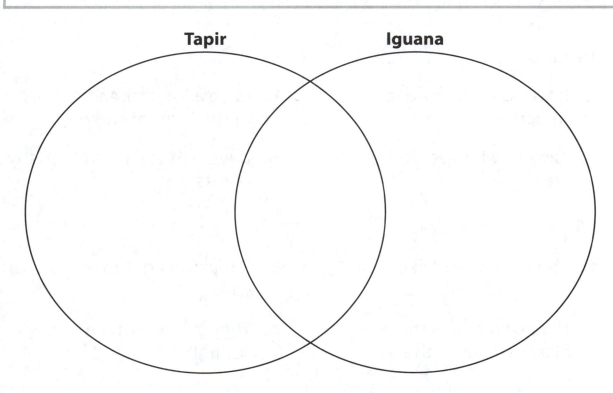

Tapir   **Iguana**

1. What can you do to find out more about these creatures?

_____

_____

Communicating Results

Learning Content

Name: _____ Date: _____

Directions: Read the text, and answer the questions.

It's Cold Out There

A tundra is a very cold climate. Plants and animals that live there need to be able to survive the cold. These areas often look icy and snowy. They are usually dry. They don't get much precipitation, which is rain or snow. These climates tend to have frozen soil. This means that few plants can grow.

1. Tundras _____ .

   a. have soil that is never frozen

   b. have a lot of precipitation in the form of snow

   c. have low temperatures and are dry

   d. have rich soil to grow many plants

2. Why are tundras dry?

   a. They have sand like deserts.

   b. They don't get much rain or snow.

   c. They don't have many plants growing there.

   d. They get too much sunlight.

3. Why are there few plants in a tundra?

   a. The soil is often frozen.

   b. The soil is never frozen.

   c. The soil has too many rocks.

   d. Animals eat all the plants.

Analyzing Data

Name: _____ **Date:** _____

Directions: There are similarities between tundras and deserts. Study the diagram. Then, answer the questions.

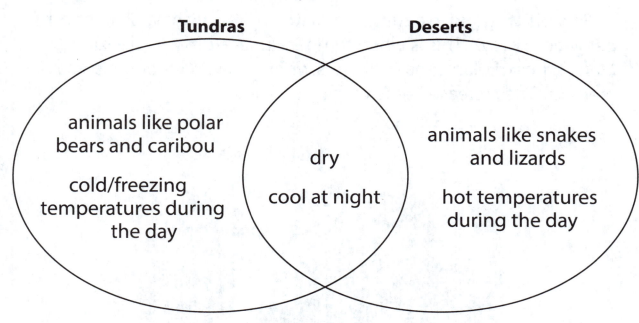

Tundras   **Deserts**

animals like polar bears and caribou

cold/freezing temperatures during the day

dry

cool at night

animals like snakes and lizards

hot temperatures during the day

1. How are tundras and deserts similar?

   a. They are both freezing during the day.

   b. They are both hot during the day.

   c. They are both dry climates.

   d. They don't have any similarities.

2. Which climate tends to have larger animals?

   a. desert

   b. tundra

   c. The animals are the same.

   d. Neither climate has animals.

3. Why might animals in deserts wait until night time to hunt?

   _____

   _____

Developing Questions

Name: _____ **Date:** _____

Directions: Read the text, and answer the questions.

> Few plants grow in a tundra climate. They only have 2–4 months per year to grow. This is when temperatures are above freezing. Many types of plants make flowers within a few days of the snow melting. They release seeds within 4–6 weeks.
>
>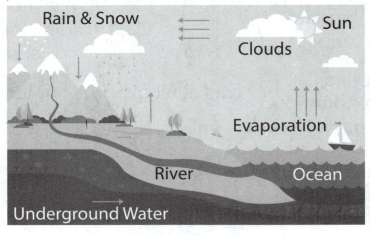

1. Why do so few plants grow in tundra climates?

   a. Plants can grow all year long.

   b. Plants cannot grow most of the year.

   c. Plants can only grow when it is snowy.

   d. Plants in tundra get too much sun.

2. Plants in the tundra produce seeds quickly so they can reproduce before _____ .

   a. wind stops blowing

   b. temperatures rise again

   c. temperatures drop again

   d. animals eat all the plants

3. What question can you ask about plants in the tundra?

   _____

   _____

Name: _____ **Date:** _____

Directions: Read the text, and answer the questions.

Keith reads about a cold climate called the tundra. He learns that there is something called permafrost. It is a layer of soil that stays frozen. Keith finds out that some plants can survive here because they have roots that go very deep in the ground to find liquid water.

1. How is permafrost different from the ground in warmer areas?

   a. There are more plants.   **b.** It stays frozen.

   c. It has more snow.   **d.** It thaws more quickly.

2. Why couldn't a plant with shallow roots survive in tundra?

   a. There is too much water in the soil.   **b.** There is too much sunlight.

   c. The roots can't reach liquid water.   **d.** There is not enough sunlight.

3. How can Keith find out how plants grow in permafrost?

   _____

   _____

   _____

   _____

Name: _____ **Date:** _____

Directions: You are designing a vehicle that will work well in cold climates. Answer the questions. Then, draw and label your vehicle.

1. What special conditions in cold climates do you need to keep in mind?

   _____

   _____

   _____

2. How will your vehicle design work with these conditions? What special features will it have?

   _____

   _____

   _____

Name: _____ **Date:** _____

Directions: Read the text, and answer the questions.

In the Comfort Zone

Climate is the weather in an area over long periods of time. There are places that have very cold climates. There are also places with very hot and dry climates. Then there are places that have warm and wet climates. A temperate climate is right in the middle of all these different climates. A temperate climate gets warm and also gets cold. It gets rain and snow at different times of the year. This kind of climate isn't dry, and it's not too wet either.

Learning Content

1. A temperate climate _____ .

   a. has no cold weather

   b. has plants that need to survive in dry areas

   c. has both warm and cold weather

   d. has very hot temperatures most of the year

2. How much precipitation does a temperate climate receive?

   a. Not much; it's dry there.

   b. A moderate amount; it gets some rain and snow.

   c. A lot; it rains almost every day.

   d. It doesn't get any.

3. What is climate?

   a. daily changes in temperature

   b. how much rain an area gets in a week

   c. the amount of daylight each day

   d. weather in an area over long periods of time

Analyzing Data

Name: _____ Date: _____

Directions: The chart compares temperatures and precipitation for different climates. Study the chart, and answer the questions.

	Temperate Climate	Desert	Tundra	Rainforest
hot temperature		X		X
cold temperature	X		X	
hot and cold temperatures	X			
regular precipitation	X			X
dry		X	X	

1. Which climate is cold and dry?

   a. temperate   **b.** desert

   c. tundra   **d.** rainforest

2. Which climate has a variety of temperatures?

   a. temperate   **b.** desert

   c. tundra   **d.** rainforest

3. The desert is the only climate that is _____.

   a. hot and wet   **b.** hot and dry

   c. cold and dry   **d.** cold and wet

Name: _____ **Date:** _____

Directions: Read the text, and answer the questions.

There are different climates in the world. They can have different temperatures. They can also have different amounts of rain and snow. Desert climates are often hot and dry. Tundras are cold and dry. Temperate climates are both warm and cold. They get rain and snow.

1. Which question would you ask to determine the kind of climate a place has?

   a. What time does the sun rise?

   b. What kind of temperatures are there all year?

   c. How many cloudy days were there this month?

   d. How many people live in the area?

2. Which of the following would tell you that a place has a temperate climate?

   a. hot temperatures all year

   b. cold temperatures all year

   c. daily rain all year

   d. a mix of warm and cold temperatures

3. Write a question that you could ask to find out more about temperate climates.

   _____

   _____

   _____

Planning Solutions

Name: _____ **Date:** _____

Directions: Read the text, and answer the questions.

> Allison wants to know what climate her grandparents live in. She visits them in the summer. The temperatures are warm and sometimes hot. There are summer thunderstorms. Her grandparents say it is cooler in the fall. They say the winter is cold with some snow.

1. Do Allison's grandparents live in a desert?

    a. Yes, deserts are cool and rainy.

    b. No, deserts are hot and dry.

    c. Yes, deserts are cold and snowy.

    d. No, deserts are hot and rainy.

2. What can Allison do to find out what climate her grandparents live in?

    a. Compare her information to other climates.

    b. Find out the climate where she lives.

    c. Record the time of sunrise each day.

    d. Study desert climate.

3. What is the next step that Allison can take to determine the climate where her grandparents live?

_____

_____

Name: _____ Date: _____

Directions: Read the text. Complete the plan for Aaron's presentation.

ABC

> Aaron is doing a project on temperate climates. He needs to learn about this climate to do his work.

1. What are two pieces of information that Aaron should be sure to include about temperate climates?

_____

_____

_____

2. What are three reliable sources of information that Aaron can use for his project?

_____

_____

_____

3. Why did you choose these sources?

_____

_____

_____

_____

_____

Communicating Results

Learning Content

Name: _____ Date: _____

Directions: Read the text, and answer the questions.

When Things Are Underwater

Flooding is a natural disaster. It can be caused by heavy rainfall. For areas near lakes, rivers, or oceans, this can cause the water level to rise.
The rising water spills over to the nearby land. Flooding can also happen if the ground can't absorb rain fast enough. People try to prepare for floods. This helps to keep them safe. It also reduces the damage caused by flooding.

1. Flooding is _____ .

    a. caused by humans using too much water

    b. a disaster that occurs only in dry areas

    c. a natural disaster

    d. caused by freezing lakes

2. What is one cause of flooding?

    a. tornados

    b. heavy rainfall

    c. blizzards

    d. frozen rivers

3. It is important to _____ .

    a. let areas flood during heavy rain

    b. make sure rain gets to nearby lakes and rivers

    c. store rainwater

    d. prepare for flooding

Name: _____ **Date:** _____

Directions: Study the chart, and answer the questions.

Structure	Definition
retaining walls	Sturdy, permanent structures that limit how high flood water rises. They divert water around buildings or other areas.
sandbags	Used temporarily to divert water around buildings or other areas. Can be placed where they are needed.
dams	Dams capture floodwater and release it slowly or divert it for other uses.
flood control channel	Empty basins that capture floodwater and drain the water into rivers or other bodies of water.

1. Retaining walls can _____ .

   a. be built from weak materials

   b. prevent heavy rain

   c. be moved when needed

   d. limit how high water rises

2. Sandbags can be placed _____ .

   a. in a permanent location

   b. where it is dry

   c. where they are needed

   d. where it doesn't flood

3. How can scientists to find out how a retaining wall will work?

   a. Wait for a flood to happen.

   b. Build a model and test it.

   c. Build a wall in a different area.

   d. Use sandbags to see how they work first.

Analyzing Data

Developing Questions

Name: _____ **Date:** _____

Directions: Read the text, and answer the questions.

> Rex builds a model of a river. He puts a layer of damp sand on a board. He builds hills and valleys in the sand. Then he tilts the board and puts one end in a pan. He slowly pours water from a spot at a top of the board to show a river flowing through the sand.

1. What could happen if Rex pours the water too quickly?

   a. There will be more hills of sand at the top.

   b. The sand will stick better to the board.

   c. Some areas will flood.

   d. Nothing different will happen.

2. What would happen if Rex added a dam to his river?

   a. It would increase flooding.

   b. It would hold back water.

   c. It would create a second river.

   d. It would increase the flow of water.

3. What is a question Rex can ask about flood control?

   _____

   _____

   _____

Name: _____ **Date:** _____

Directions: Read the text. Then, answer the questions.

One way to protect against flood damage is to use sandbags. Bags are partially filled with sand or soil. Then they are stacked on top of each other. They form a barrier that diverts water around buildings. They can be used most anywhere. The wall of sandbags should not be stacked higher than two or three bags high, or it might collapse.

1. A limitation of sandbags is _____.

    a. they are too expensive to make

    b. they are too difficult to make

    c. they can be stacked most anywhere

    d. they can only be stacked to a certain height

2. Sandbags are not helpful _____.

    a. if the flood waters are too high

    b. if it is raining

    c. if they are stacked on each other

    d. if it is windy

3. What could you do if you wanted to find a way to improve sandbags?

_____

_____

Name: _____ **Date:** _____

Directions: Study the chart, and answer the questions.

Retaining Wall	Sandbag
permanent structure	inexpensive to make
can be built to be different heights	can be used most anywhere
can be built from strong materials, like concrete	can only be stacked to a certain height

1. Which would work best to protect a house in an area where it often floods? Explain your answer.

   _____

   _____

   _____

2. In what situation might someone choose to use sandbags? Why?

   _____

   _____

   _____

Name: _____ Date: _____

Directions: Read the text, and answer the questions.

Just Add Salt

Some areas have freezing temperatures during winter. This can make roads very slippery. Snow plows clear the roads and scatter salt onto the road. Why salt? Water freezes at 0 °C (32 °F). When water is mixed with salt, it lowers the temperature at which it freezes. This means that it melts ice and stops water from freezing.

Learning Content

1. Why is salt used on icy roads?

   a. It makes water freeze at a higher temperature.

   b. It makes water freeze at a lower temperature.

   c. It provides less traction on ice.

   d. It warms the road so ice can't form.

2. What might happen if not enough salt is put on the roads?

   a. There would be icy patches on the roads.

   b. The snow would build up more slowly.

   c. The plows would have to do less work.

   d. There would be no ice on the roads.

3. Salt will not work as well _____ .

   a. on roads that have been plowed

   b. when it isn't going to snow

   c. when it has stopped snowing

   d. on unplowed roads

Analyzing Data

Name: _____ **Date:** _____

Directions: Salt changes the freezing point of water. The more salt, the higher the freezing temperature. The graph shows the freezing point of water and water with two different salt mixtures. Study the graph, and the questions.

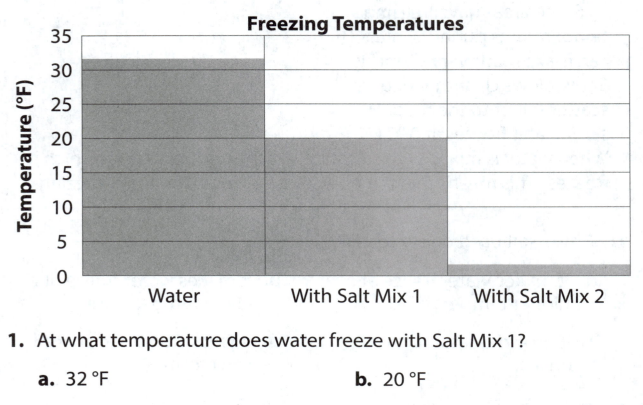

1. At what temperature does water freeze with Salt Mix 1?

   a. 32 °F   **b.** 20 °F

   c. 5 °F   **d.** 2 °F

2. At what temperature does water freeze with Salt Mix 2?

   a. 32 °F   **b.** 20 °F

   c. 12 °F   **d.** 2 °F

3. Salt Mix 1 _____ .

   a. has more salt in it than   **b.** has less water in it than
        Salt Mix 2   Salt Mix 2

   c. has less salt in it than   **d.** has an equal amount of
        Salt Mix 2   salt as Salt Mix 2

Name: _____ **Date:** _____

Directions: Read the text, and answer the questions.

Hailey is walking on the sidewalk. It has a lot of snow covering it. Hailey notices that there are small holes in the snow. She sees that salt has been scattered there. It didn't melt all everything because there was too much snow.

Developing Questions

1. Why did the salt only make small holes in the snow?

   a. There is too much snow.

   b. The temperatures are too warm.

   c. Too much salt was used.

   d. There was no ice on the sidewalk.

2. What question would help you decide if the salt is working?

   a. Is it still snowing?

   b. How much salt was used?

   c. Is the sidewalk snowy or icy?

   d. How wide is the sidewalk?

3. Write a question you have about how salt works with ice.

   _____

   _____

Name: _____ **Date:** _____

Directions: Read the text, and look at the chart. Answer the questions.

Derek is doing an investigation. He has three ice cubes that are the same size. He puts them in a large pan, separate from each other. He leaves one ice cube alone. He sprinkles salt on one and an equal amount of sand on the other. The chart shows Derek's observations after 15 minutes.

Ice Cube 1	plain	melting a bit
Ice Cube 2	salt	almost all melted
Ice Cube 3	sand	melted as much as the plain cube

1. Based on this, which would be most helpful to melt ice on sidewalks and roads?

   a. putting sand on the ice   **b.** leaving the ice alone

   c. putting salt on the ice   **d.** none of these

2. Which is melting the fastest?

   a. Ice Cube 1   **b.** Ice Cube 2

   c. Ice Cube 3   **d.** Ice Cubes 2 and 3 are melting at the same rate

3. How can Derek test to see if more salt would make the ice melt faster?

   _____

   _____

   _____

Planning Solutions

Name: _____ **Date:** _____

Directions: This graph shows the number of car accidents that happened in one city during winter. Study the graph, and answer the questions.

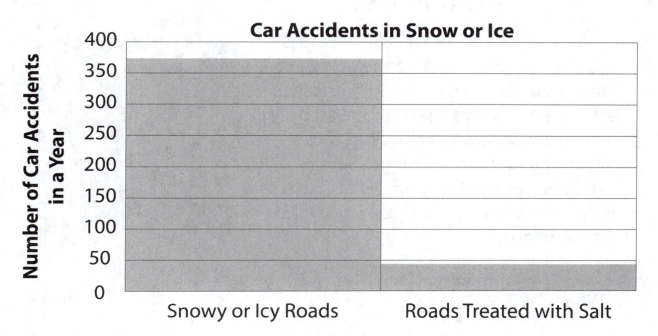

Car Accidents in Snow or Ice

Number of Car Accidents in a Year

400
350
300
250
200
150
100
50
0

Snowy or Icy Roads   Roads Treated with Salt

Road Conditions

1. Describe the difference between the number of accidents that happened on roads treated with salt and those that happened on untreated roads.

   _____

   _____

   _____

2. It costs the city a lot of money to salt roads. Accidents cause injuries, death, traffic condition, and damage to roadways. Is it worth it for the city to salt the roads? Why or why not?

   _____

   _____

Name: _____ **Date:** _____

Directions: Read the text, and answer the questions.

Blown Away!

Wind is part of our weather. Wind is moving air. It can be a gentle breeze or stormy winds. Tornados and hurricanes are types of storms that have very strong winds. These strong winds can cause a lot of damage to buildings. Some buildings are built with materials, such as reinforced concrete, that can withstand strong winds.

1. What is wind?

   a. tornados   **b.** moving air

   c. hurricanes   **d.** rain

2. The materials used for buildings _____ .

   a. help them to avoid strong   **b.** can cause a tornado
   winds

   c. can keep them from being   **d.** do not help in strong winds
   damaged by wind

3. What kind of building material could withstand strong wind?

   a. reinforced concrete   **b.** wood

   c. shingles   **d.** drywall

51409—180 Days of Science   © Shell Education

Name: _____ **Date:** _____

Directions: Read the text, study the chart, and answer the questions.

> There is a scale that is used to help scientists study tornados and the damage that they do. The higher the wind speed, the greater damage it causes.

Tornado Category	Estimated Wind Speed (kilometers per hour)
EF0	105–137
EF1	138–177
EF2	178–217
EF3	218–266
EF4	267–322
EF5	>322

1. Which tornado causes the most damage?

    a. EF2   **b.** EF3

    c. EF4   **d.** EF5

2. A tornado with a wind speed of 323 kph is an _____ .

    a. EF0   **b.** EF2

    c. EF4   **d.** EF5

3. How does an EF3 tornado compare to an EF1?

_____

_____

Developing Questions

Name: _____   Date: _____

Directions: Read the text, and answer the questions.

Wendy's little brother has a sandbox. It has a lid for when it is not being used. After a windy storm, Wendy sees that the sandbox is missing its lid. The lid is laying in the middle of the yard.

1. What does the lid tell about the weather?

    a. There were heavy rains during the storm.

    b. The wind was strong enough to blow off the lid.

    c. It was sunny after the storm.

    d. The temperature was warmer after the rain.

2. Which question will help Wendy find a way to keep the lid on?

    a. How will placing something heavy on the lid help?

    b. How much sand should be in the sandbox?

    c. How can the sand be kept dry?

    d. Can the wind blow away the sand?

3. Write a question that you have about the effects of wind.

    _____

    _____

    _____

Name: _____ **Date:** _____

Directions: Read the text. Then, answer the questions.

Darren is building a model of a house. He wants it to withstand wind from a hair dryer. He is trying different materials. The chart shows the materials he used and what happened when he used the hair dryer to simulate strong wind.

Material	Observation
paper	blows away
fabric	blows away
cardboard	moves a little
wood	stays in place, doesn't move

1. Which material should Darren use?

   a. paper   **b.** fabric

   c. cardboard   **d.** wood

2. The materials that are least sturdy_____ .

   a. blow away   **b.** stay in place

   c. move a little   **d.** are the easiest to paint

3. What are some other materials that Darren could use to build his model house?

   _____

   _____

   _____

Planning Solutions

Communicating Results

Name: _____ **Date:** _____

Directions: Read the text, and answer the questions.

> Different types of roofs withstand wind better than others. Hipped roofs perform better in windstorms than most gabled roofs. Roofs that are properly attached to the exterior walls are less likely to blow off.

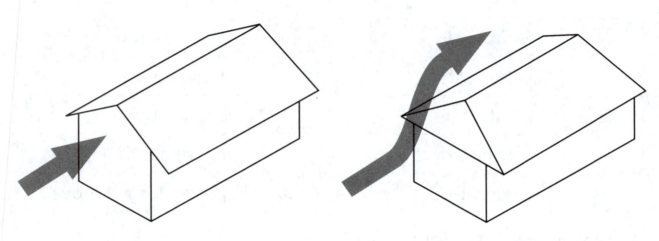

Gabled Roof   **Hipped Roof**

1. Why do you think that a hipped roof performs better in windstorms?

_____

_____

_____

2. Why should roofs be attached to exterior walls?

_____

_____

_____

Name: _____ **Date:** _____

Directions: Read the text, and answer the questions.

Screening Out the Sun

The sun is important for life on Earth to exist. Too much sun can be harmful, though. It can cause sunburns and skin cancer. Sunburn can happen even on cold days. One way to protect skin is by using sunscreen. It has ingredients that reflect and absorb the damaging rays of the sun. Sunscreens have ratings, such as SPF 15 or SPF 30. The higher the SPF number is, the more protection it provides from the sun.

Learning Content

1. Which of the following sunscreens provide the most protection?

   a. SPF 15   **b.** SPF 20

   c. SPF 30   **d.** SPF 45

2. Why is it important to wear sunscreen?

   a. to keep skin cool   **b.** to help avoid sunburn

   c. to help skin stay soft   **d.** to keep from sweating

3. On cold days, _____ .

   a. you still need to wear sunscreen
   b. you don't need to wear sunscreen

   c. sunscreen is not effective
   d. your skin doesn't get hot enough to need sunscreen

Analyzing Data

Name: _____ **Date:** _____

Directions: There are different ways to protect yourself from the sun. Study the chart, and answer the questions.

Protection	Description and Effects
clothing	Clothing helps block some of the sun's rays.
sunscreen	Sunscreen with at least SPF 15 blocks most of the sun's rays. It can be applied to all exposed skin.
hats	Wide-brim hats (not baseball caps) protect the neck, ears, eyes, forehead, nose, and scalp.
sunglasses	Protects eyes from the sun's rays.
limiting sun exposure	Limits your exposure to the sun's rays. They are most intense between 10:00 a.m. and 4:00 p.m.

1. Which can be used to protect all of your skin?

   a. hat

   b. sunglasses

   c. clothing

   d. sunscreen

2. Which one gives your face and neck the best protection from the sun?

   a. long sleeve shirt

   b. baseball cap

   c. sunglasses

   d. wide-brimmed hat

3. If you want to avoid the most intense sun rays, when would be a good time to go outside? Why?

   _____

   _____

   _____

Name: _____ **Date:** _____

Directions: Read the text, and answer the questions.

> Jason wants to see how sunscreen works. He takes a piece of black construction paper and draws a line down the middle of it. He applies sunscreen to one side of the paper and does nothing to the other side. He takes it outside and leaves it in the sun. When he brings it inside, he sees that the side with the sunscreen is still black. The other side with no protection is faded.

1. The side with sunscreen _____ .

    a. stayed black

    b. faded in the sun

    c. was not protected from the sun's rays

    d. was hotter than the other side

2. What does the faded side show?

    a. the real color of the paper

    b. the protection of the sunscreen

    c. the damage the sun can do

    d. the temperature in the sunlight

3. Write a question that Jason can ask to find out more about sunscreen.

    _____

    _____

    _____

Name: _____ **Date:** _____

Directions: Read the text. Study the chart, and answer the questions.

Claire is testing different SPFs using UV beads. The beads are white inside and turn blue when they are in sunlight. She puts some beads in four small, clear plastic bags. She puts a different sunscreen on the outside of each of three bags. She doesn't put anything on the outside of the fourth bag. She takes the bags and puts them in the sun.

Bag	Sunscreen	Color of Beads
#1	none	dark blue
#2	SPF 15	blue
#3	SPF 30	light blue
#4	SPF 45	very light blue

1. What color are the beads that were most protected?

   a. dark blue   **b.** blue

   c. light blue   **d.** very light blue

2. You want the most protection from the sun. You should_____ .

   a. wear SPF 15 sunscreen   **b.** wear SPF 30 sunscreen

   c. wear SPF 45 sunscreen   **d.** do nothing

3. What should Claire do if she wants to find out more about sunscreen protection?

   _____

   _____

Name: _____ **Date:** _____

Directions: Draw a picture of how you'd protect yourself from sun. Label your picture, and answer the question.

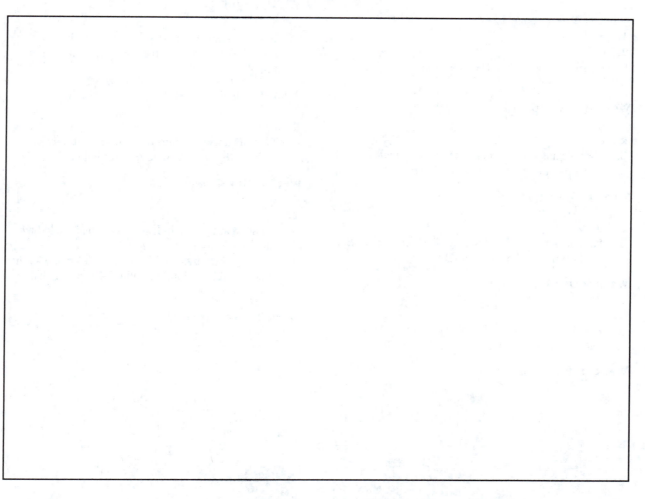

1. How can you choose sunscreen that will give you the most protection?

_____

_____

2. What do you think is the most important way to protect your skin from sun damage? Why?

_____

_____

Answer Key

Life Science

Week 1: Day 1 (page 14)
1. d
2. d
3. Possible answer includes, "The animal might get hurt."

Week 1: Day 2 (page 15)
1. c
2. d
3. Possible answer includes, "It is easier to talk about a group when it has a name of its own."

Week 1: Day 3 (page 16)
1. a
2. b
3. Possible answer includes, "Does it help lions to find food when they live together?"

Week 1: Day 4 (page 17)
1. d
2. d
3. Possible answer includes, "He could try adding a plastic fish to see what happens."

Week 1: Day 5 (page 18)

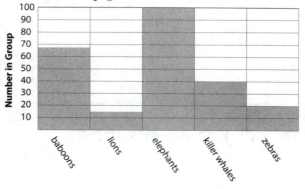

1. Elephants, lions.

Week 2: Day 1 (page 19)
1. a
2. a
3. Possible answer includes, "They need to make sure that there is enough food for the whole group."

Week 2: Day 2 (page 20)
1. d
2. b
3. Possible answer includes, "They can collect more food if there are more baboons doing the same thing."

Week 2: Day 3 (page 21)
1. d
2. a
3. Possible answer includes, "How does it help the animals to stand in circle for protection?"

Week 2: Day 4 (page 22)
1. a
2. c
3. Possible answer includes, "The animal could have claws to fight off enemies."
4. Possible drawing should include at least one feature that would be helpful to defend the group, like claws.

Week 2: Day 5 (page 23)

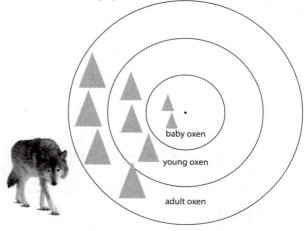

1. Possible answer includes, "The babies need the most protection, so they need to be in the center of the circle."

Week 3: Day 1 (page 24)
1. b
2. b
3. Possible answer includes, "The seeds fall to the ground near the parent plant."

Answer Key (cont.)

Week 3: Day 2 (page 25)
1. c
2. b
3. fruit stage

Week 3: Day 3 (page 26)
1. a
2. d
3. Possible answer includes, "How many tomatoes does each flower bud produce?"

Week 3: Day 4 (page 27)
1. b
2. b
3. Possible answer includes, "Plant the seeds at different times."

Week 3: Day 5 (page 28)

	Seeds on the Left (Sunny Side)	Seeds on the Right (Shady Side)
time to sprout	3 days	5 days
color of seedlings	bright green	pale green
plant's size at the end of the month	5 inches	3 inches

1. Possible answer includes, "The amount of sunlight because that is the difference between the two plants."

Week 4: Day 1 (page 29)
1. a
2. a
3. Baby, juvenile, adult

Week 4: Day 2 (page 30)
1. b
2. a
3. Possible answer includes, "A dog because it needs to nurse."

Week 4: Day 3 (page 31)
1. d
2. b
3. Possible answer includes, "Does a mother turtle take care of her babies?"

Week 4: Day 4 (page 32)
1. b
2. d
3. Possible answer includes, "The zookeeper can keep one alligator in a smaller exhibit and place another alligator in a larger exhibit."

Week 4: Day 5 (page 33)

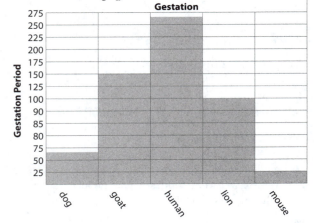

1. Longest—goat; shortest—mouse

Week 5: Day 1 (page 34)
1. c
2. d
3. Possible answer includes, "They study fossils to learn about plants and animals that used to live on Earth."

Week 5: Day 2 (page 35)
1. c
2. d
3. Possible answer includes, "The animal dies. The sot parts rot. The bones are covered in mud and sediments."

Week 5: Day 3 (page 36)
1. a
2. d
3. Possible answer includes, "Does where it was found tell me anything about the habitat of this fossil?"

Week 5: Day 4 (page 37)
1. a
2. b
3. Possible answer includes, "She could look to see if it has any structures that would help it to live in water."

Week 5: Day 5 (page 38)
A fish dies.; Its body sinks to the bottom of the water.; Soft parts rot.; Mud covers the bones.; Sand and sediments make layers.; Bones turn to stone.

Answer Key (cont.)

Week 6: Day 1 (page 39)
1. a
2. c
3. a

Week 6: Day 2 (page 40)
1. b
2. d
3. Possible answers include, "Dragonflies and fish."

Week 6: Day 3 (page 41)
1. d
2. c
3. Possible answer includes, "What do its structures tell about its habitat?"

Week 6: Day 4 (page 42)
1. d
2. a
3. Possible answer includes, "Look at the main structures of the fossil and see if there is a living thing that has similar structures."

Week 6: Day 5 (page 43)
Possible answers include:
Fossil #1: It has a long tail and spikes
Fossil #2: it looks like a fish
Middle of Venn diagram: They both look like sea creatures. They both have tails.

Week 7: Day 1 (page 44)
1. c
2. a
3. Possible answers include, "food, water, shelter."

Week 7: Day 2 (page 45)
1. b
2. d
3. b

Week 7: Day 3 (page 46)
1. c
2. a
3. Possible answer includes, "Can camouflage help predators get prey?"

Week 7: Day 4 (page 47)
1. a
2. b
3. Possible answer includes, "I would give it waterproof fur and claws to dig burrows to keep cool in the summer. My animal would have wings to migrate for the cold winters."

Week 7: Day 5 (page 48)
Arctic fox—Camouflage helps it avoid predators.
Penguin—Thick layer of fat keeps it warm.
Mountain goat—Hooves help it climb rocks
Fish—Gills help it breathe underwater.
Camel—Humps allow it to store energy.

Week 8: Day 1 (page 49)
1. d
2. a
3. a

Week 8: Day 2 (page 50)
1. a
2. a
3. c

Week 8: Day 3 (page 51)
1. d
2. a
3. Possible answer includes, "How can we help baby sea turtles find the ocean?"

Week 8: Day 4 (page 52)
1. c
2. a
3. Possible answer includes, "She could observe the food supply for the ducks."

Week 8: Day 5 (page 53)

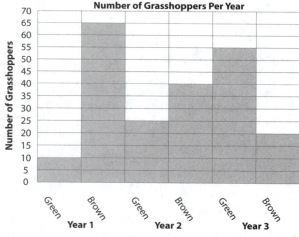

Week 9: Day 1 (page 54)
1. a
2. c
3. c

Answer Key (cont.)

Week 9: Day 2 (page 55)
1. a
2. c
3. a

Week 9: Day 3 (page 56)
1. b
2. d
3. Possible answer includes, "How much will the puppies look like the parents?"

Week 9: Day 4 (page 57)
1. b
2. a
3. Possible answer includes, "He could record the number and the color of flowers each plant produces."

Week 9: Day 5 (page 58)
Students should circle: tall, brown eyes, curly hair, and dark skin.
1. Possible answer includes, "Yes, because traits are inherited from both parents."

Week 10: Day 1 (page 59)
1. a
2. b
3. d

Week 10: Day 2 (page 60)
1. c
2. b
3. b

Week 10: Day 3 (page 61)
1. c
2. b
3. Possible answer includes, "Do all sea otters use rocks to open shells?"

Week 10: Day 4 (page 62)
1. c
2. b
3. Possible answer includes, "Olivia could try giving Plant #1 the same amount of water as Plant #2."

Week 10: Day 5 (page 63)
Chart: There is not enough rain.—Plants start to die; Trees are cut down—Squirrels move to a different part of the forest.; Winter begins—The fur on the Arctic fox turns white.
1. Possible answer includes, "The sun shines, and the rain puddles dry up."

Week 11: Day 1 (page 64)
1. b
2. d
3. a

Week 11: Day 2 (page 65)
1. a
2. d
3. c

Week 11: Day 3 (page 66)
1. c
2. b
3. Possible answer includes, "Are males and females different sizes?"

Week 11: Day 4 (page 67)
1. d
2. a
3. Possible answer includes, "Observe how a slender ferret can fit in a small hole compared to a fatter ferret."

Week 11: Day 5 (page 68)
Students should draw two of the same kind of animal. One drawing should show at least one variation.
1. Answers will vary. Students should describe how the variation(s) could help or hurt the animal.

Week 12: Day 1 (page 69)
1. c
2. d
3. a
4. Possible answer includes, "Find a new tree to live in."

Week 12: Day 2 (page 70)
1. a
2. a
3. Possible answer includes, "No, because they would have the food they need without migrating."

Week 12: Day 3 (page 71)
1. a
2. b
3. Possible answer includes, "Where did the disease come from?"

Week 12: Day 4 (page 72)
1. a
2. d
3. Possible answer includes, "Derek would need to see if the number of monarch butterflies increases."

Answer Key *(cont.)*

Week 12: Day 5 (page 73)
1. Possible answer includes a drawing of a planted field with labels.
2. Possible answer includes, "This is a good solution because the roots of the plants will hold the soil in place."

Physical Science

Week 1: Day 1 (page 74)
1. a
2. b
3. d

Week 1: Day 2 (page 75)
1. c
2. a
3. Possible answer includes, "He could lift more water with his friend than he could alone."

Week 1: Day 3 (page 76)
1. b
2. d
3. Possible answer includes, "Is it easier to pull the wagon when nothing is in it?"

Week 1: Day 4 (page 77)
1. c
2. a
3. Possible answer includes, "He could try using different amounts of force to see how fast the sled goes."

Week 1: Day 5 (page 78)
The first picture should be circled.
1. Possible answer includes, "Because the wagon would be heavier with things in it. This would require more force."
2. Possible answer includes, "It would require more force to move it."
3. Possible answer includes, "Yes, because they would weigh the same amount."

Week 2: Day 1 (page 79)
1. d
2. a
3. c

Week 2: Day 2 (page 80)
1. a
2. c
3. Possible answer includes, "The speed of the ball increases with the height of the ramp."

Week 2: Day 3 (page 81)
1. d
2. c
3. Possible answer includes, "How does kicking it gently affect how far it will go?"

Week 2: Day 4 (page 82)
1. b
2. a
3. Possible answer includes, "She could try pushing snowballs up different hills."

Week 2: Day 5 (page 83)
1. Student drawing should show a track with a steeper hill.
2. Possible answer includes, "Faster because it is heavier."

Week 3: Day 1 (page 84)
1. b
2. a
3. c
4. Possible answer includes, "The empty box is easier to push."

Week 3: Day 2 (page 85)
1. b
2. d
3. Possible answer includes, "Vert hard because the cart would be heavy."

Week 3: Day 3 (page 86)
1. d
2. c
3. Possible answer includes, "How fast will the sled go with a gentle push?"

Week 3: Day 4 (page 87)
1. c
2. b
3. Possible answer includes, "She can pack less in each box."

Answer Key (cont.)

Week 3: Day 5 (page 88)

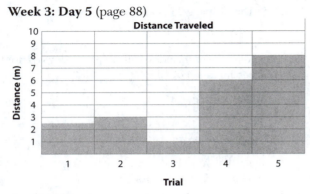

1. Trial #5

Week 4: Day 1 (page 89)
1. b
2. d
3. a

Week 4: Day 2 (page 90)
1. a
2. c
3. Possible answer includes, "Put three 50 g weights and one 100 g weight on the left and one 250 g weight on the right."

Week 4: Day 3 (page 91)
1. a
2. a
3. Possible answer could include, "Will the seesaw go faster if I sit closer to the middle?"

Week 4: Day 4 (page 92)
1. c
2. a
3. Possible answer includes, "Remove cookies from one package until it is tilting to one side."

Week 4: Day 5 (page 93)
1. Possible answer includes, "They are taking turns pushing off the ground."
2. Possible answer includes, "The seesaw goes up and down on alternating sides."
3. Possible answer includes, "The seesaw would not move. It would lean to the side of the heaver person."

Week 5: Day 1 (page 94)
1. d
2. b
3. c

Week 5: Day 2 (page 95)
1. c
2. a
3. b

Week 5: Day 3 (page 96)
1. b
2. c
3. Possible answer includes, "How much force is needed to go 4 feet forward?"

Week 5: Day 4 (page 97)
1. d
2. b
3. Possible answer includes, "He could change the chain length and time how long it takes to go back and forth 10 times using the same amount of force each time."

Week 5: Day 5 (page 98)
Students should add arrows to the diagram that show the bird feeder will swing in the direction that the squirrel pushes it.
1. Possible answer includes, "The bird house will swing in the same direction that the squirrel pushes it because that is the direction of the force."

Week 6: Day 1 (page 99)
1. a
2. d
3. c

Week 6: Day 2 (page 100)
1. c
2. a
3. b
4. d

Week 6: Day 3 (page 101)
1. c
2. b
3. Possible answer includes, "How can I attach the arrow so that it will spin quickly?"

Week 6: Day 4 (page 102)
1. b
2. a
3. Possible answer includes, "He can compare the force needed to push an empty merry-go-round and one with people on it."

Answer Key (cont.)

Week 6: Day 5 (page 103)

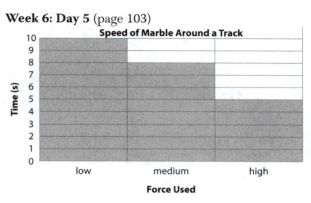

Week 7: Day 1 (page 104)
1. c
2. a
3. b

Week 7: Day 2 (page 105)
1. a
2. b
3. a

Week 7: Day 3 (page 106)
1. b
2. c
3. Possible answer includes, "What is the longest time a balloon will stick to the wall with static electricity?"

Week 7: Day 4 (page 107)
1. b
2. a
3. Possible answer includes, "Try rubbing the balloons on different materials."

Week 7: Day 5 (page 108)
Students should draw one picture with the balloon close to their hair and their hair standing tall. The other picture should show the balloon further away, and their hair should not be standing up as much.

Week 8: Day 1 (page 109)
1. d
2. c
3. a

Week 8: Day 2 (page 110)
1. a
2. c
3. a

Week 8: Day 3 (page 111)
1. c
2. b
3. Possible answer includes, "How does a compass use magnetism to tell direction?"

Week 8: Day 4 (page 112)
1. b
2. c
3. Possible answer includes, "She should use the magnet that gets close to the ring because the magnetic force will be stronger."

Week 8: Day 5 (page 113)

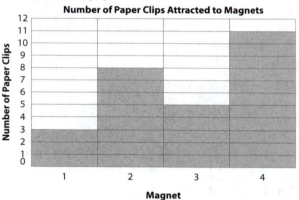

1. Possible answer includes, "Magnet #4 is the strongest because it attracted the most paper clips."

Week 9: Day 1 (page 114)
1. d
2. c
3. d

Week 9: Day 2 (page 115)
1. a
2. b
3. d

Week 9: Day 3 (page 116)
1. b
2. c
3. Possible answer includes, "Does the amount of rubbing the clothes together increase the amount of static cling?"

Week 9: Day 4 (page 117)
1. b
2. c
3. Possible answer includes, "The clothes would come apart easily because the static cling will be reduced."

Answer Key *(cont.)*

Week 9: Day 5 (page 118)

Students should draw a "before" picture that shows that the paper is not attracted to the rod. The "after" picture should show paper clinging to the rod.

1. Possible answer includes, "The paper does not cling to the rod at first because there is no static electricity. The wool charges the rod with static electricity, so the paper clings to it."

Week 10: Day 1 (page 119)

1. c
2. a
3. d

Week 10: Day 2 (page 120)

1. a
2. b
3. d
4. Possible answer includes, "Type 2 because homes are not very hot or very cold."

Week 10: Day 3 (page 121)

1. c
2. b
3. Possible answer includes, "Will stronger magnets help it to clean better?"

Week 10: Day 4 (page 122)

1. b
2. d
3. Possible answer includes, "He could set up an investigation to compare liquids mixed by hand and liquids mixed by the magnetic stirrer."

Week 10: Day 5 (page 123)

1. From left to right: the magnetic poles should be s, n, n, s or n, s, s, n.
2. The student's diagram should show the toy cars with this magnet orientation: s,n,s,n or n,s,n,s.

Week 11: Day 1 (page 124)

1. c
2. b
3. d

Week 11: Day 2 (page 125)

1. b
2. a
3. a

Week 11: Day 3 (page 126)

1. d
2. a
3. Possible answer includes, "Where are the magnets placed in the door in order to keep it closed?"

Week 11: Day 4 (page 127)

1. b
2. a
3. Possible answer includes, "Use one magnet with a metal piece so that the attraction isn't as strong as it would be between two magnets."

Week 11: Day 5 (page 128)

Magnet Position	Observations	Example
Directly across from each other	They click together and the flap stays closed.	
One lower than the other	The flap closes, but is somewhat easy to open.	
5 inches apart	The flap closes, but the magnets do not hold it closed.	

1. Possible answer includes, "The magnets placed directly across from each other."

Week 12: Day 1 (page 129)

1. b
2. c
3. a

Week 12: Day 2 (page 130)

1. d
2. b
3. No, because magnets are attracted to both of them.

Week 12: Day 3 (page 131)

1. a
2. d
3. Possible answer includes, "If the attraction is increased, will it attract more of the metal?"

Answer Key *(cont.)*

Week 12: Day 4 (page 132)
1. b
2. c
3. Possible answer includes, "He can attach the magnet to a string and put it into the water where the lure is."

Week 12: Day 5 (page 133)
Student drawing should label objects on the inner ring with "strong pull" and objects on the outer ring with "weak pull."
1. Possible answer includes, "The objects that are closer to the magnet are going to have a stronger attraction to the magnet."

Earth and Space Science

Week 1: Day 1 (page 134)
1. c
2. b
3. a

Week 1: Day 2 (page 135)
1. c
2. b
3. d
4. 10 days

Week 1: Day 3 (page 136)
1. c
2. b
3. Possible answer includes, "How cold does it get in winter?"

Week 1: Day 4 (page 137)
1. b
2. a
3. Possible answer includes, "He could record the temperatures and the weather over a longer period of time."

Week 1: Day 5 (page 138)

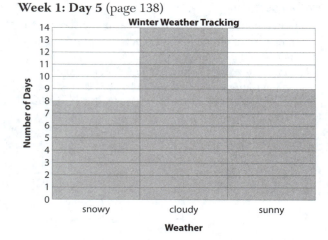

1. Possible answer includes, "The sunny days because it snows when it is cold."

Week 2: Day 1 (page 139)
1. b
2. d
3. c

Week 2: Day 2 (page 140)
1. b
2. a
3. Possible answer includes, "They would be higher because it would be summer. Temperatures in summer are higher."

Week 2: Day 3 (page 141)
1. c
2. a
3. Possible answer includes, "Does temperature affect when migrating animals return home?"

Week 2: Day 4 (page 142)
1. d
2. c
3. Possible answer includes, "She should plan the plants that will grow best where she will plant her garden."

Week 2: Day 5 (page 143)
Students can place "partly cloudy" and "rainy" in either spot.
1. Possible answer includes, "It made sense to have the rainy day go with the other rainy day."
2. Possible answer includes, "A partly cloudy day because the clouds are disappearing after the rain storm."

Answer Key *(cont.)*

Week 3: Day 1 (page 144)
1. b
2. c
3. d

Week 3: Day 2 (page 145)
1. a
2. c
3. b

Week 3: Day 3 (page 146)
1. a
2. c
3. Possible answer includes, "Does the temperature affect how much rain there is?"

Week 3: Day 4 (page 147)
1. a
2. d
3. Possible answer includes, "A thermometer could be set up in the sun and another thermometer could be set up in the shade and temperature readings could be taken on the same days at the same time."

Week 3: Day 5 (page 148)
Students should circle swimming, building sand castles, and riding a bike.
1. Possible answer includes, "These are good summer activities because they can be done outside in warm weather."

Week 4: Day 1 (page 149)
1. b
2. c
3. a

Week 4: Day 2 (page 150)
1. c
2. d
3. b

Week 4: Day 3 (page 151)
1. b
2. d
3. Possible answer could include, "How does the temperature change from morning to afternoon to night?"

Week 4: Day 4 (page 152)
1. a
2. c
3. Possible answer includes, "Find out how shorter days affects the weather."

Week 4: Day 5 (page 153)
Fall: Leaves change color, days are shorter, temperatures are cooler.
Winter: Temperatures are colder, some areas get snow.
Spring: Temperatures start to warm, plants start to grow.
Summer: Temperatures are hotter. Trees are full of leaves.
1. Possible answer includes, "The patterns help to describe the kind of temperatures and precipitation to expect during each season."

Week 5: Day 1 (page 154)
1. c
2. d
3. a

Week 5: Day 2 (page 155)
1. c
2. a
3. b

Week 5: Day 3 (page 156)
1. a
2. c
3. Possible answer includes, "How do animals survive on small amounts of water?"

Week 5: Day 4 (page 157)
1. b
2. d
3. Possible answer includes, "She should come up with a question and test it."
4. Possible answer includes, "Dry land, desert plants, desert animals."

Week 5: Day 5 (page 158)
1. Possible answer includes, "Elephant tree and saguaro cactus. It is useful because there is not much rain in the desert."
2. Possible answer includes, "To conserve energy while it does not have water available."
3. Cactus

Week 6: Day 1 (page 159)
1. b
2. a
3. d

Week 6: Day 2 (page 160)
1. c
2. a
3. b

Answer Key (cont.)

Week 6: Day 3 (page 161)
1. c
2. a
3. Possible answer includes, "What does this insect eat?"

Week 6: Day 4 (page 162)
1. b
2. c
3. Possible answer includes, "Research ways you can help save the rainforest."

Week 6: Day 5 (page 163)

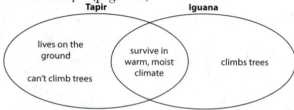

1. Possible answer includes, "Research in books, encyclopedias, and reliable websites."

Week 7: Day 1 (page 164)
1. c
2. b
3. a

Week 7: Day 2 (page 165)
1. c
2. b
3. Possible answer includes, "Because it is cooler at night."

Week 7: Day 3 (page 166)
1. b
2. c
3. Possible answer includes, "How do plants survive in the tundra?"

Week 7: Day 4 (page 167)
1. b
2. c
3. Possible answer includes, "He can find information from reliable sources."

Week 7: Day 5 (page 168)
1. Possible answer includes, "The cold temperatures and the frozen ground."
2. Answers will vary and depend on the student's design.

Week 8: Day 1 (page 169)
1. c
2. b
3. d

Week 8: Day 2 (page 170)
1. c
2. a
3. b

Week 8: Day 3 (page 171)
1. b
2. d
3. Possible answer includes, "Do the temperatures change with the seasons?"

Week 8: Day 4 (page 172)
1. b
2. a
3. Possible answer includes, "She could record the amount of precipitation to compare to temperate climate information."

Week 8: Day 5 (page 173)
1. Possible answer includes, "That there are warm and cold temperatures throughout the year and that there is rain and snow for precipitation, so the climate is not dry."
2. Possible answer may include an encyclopedia, a website that ends in .edu, a nonfiction book about different climates.
3. Possible answer includes, "I chose those sources because they have information that can be trusted to be factual."

Week 9: Day 1 (page 174)
1. c
2. b
3. d

Week 9: Day 2 (page 175)
1. d
2. c
3. b

Week 9: Day 3 (page 176)
1. c
2. b
3. Possible answer includes, "What are some other things that can control flood water?"

Answer Key *(cont.)*

Week 9: Day 4 (page 177)

1. d
2. a
3. Possible answer includes, "Find their limitations and see how to make them better."

Week 9: Day 5 (page 178)

1. Possible answer includes, "A retaining wall because it is a permanent structure."
2. Possible answer includes, "In an area where it rarely floods because permanent flood barriers aren't needed."

Week 10: Day 1 (page 179)

1. b
2. a
3. d

Week 10: Day 2 (page 180)

1. b
2. d
3. a

Week 10: Day 3 (page 181)

1. a
2. c
3. Possible answer includes, "Does it matter how much salt is used on ice?"

Week 10: Day 4 (page 182)

1. b
2. c
3. Possible answer includes, "He could take several ice cubes at the same time, put different amounts of salt on them, and time them to see how long they take to melt."

Week 10: Day 5 (page 183)

1. Possible answer includes, "Many more accidents happened on the roads that were not treated with salt."
2. Possible answer includes, "Yes, because there is too much risk with leaving the roads untreated."

Week 11: Day 1 (page 184)

1. b
2. c
3. a

Week 11: Day 2 (page 185)

1. d
2. d
3. Possible answer includes, "It is stronger."

Week 11: Day 3 (page 186)

1. b
2. a
3. Possible answer includes, "How strong does wind have to blow to move a car?"

Week 11: Day 4 (page 187)

1. d
2. a
3. Possible answer includes, "Blocks, bricks, mud."

Week 11: Day 5 (page 188)

1. Possible answer includes, "Because the wind flows over it more easily."
2. Possible answer includes, "To help keep them from blowing off the building."

Week 12: Day 1 (page 189)

1. d
2. b
3. a

Week 12: Day 2 (page 190)

1. d
2. d
3. Possible answer includes, "In the early morning because the sun's rays aren't too strong yet."

Week 12: Day 3 (page 191)

1. a
2. c
3. Possible answer includes, "What would happen to the paper if I use a different SPF on each side?"

Week 12: Day 4 (page 192)

1. d
2. c
3. Possible answer includes, "Observe the beads over a few hours to see if the sunscreen stops working."

Week 12: Day 5 (page 193)

Students should draw a picture of a person using methods for sun protection, such as clothing, sunglasses, hats, and sunscreen.

1. Possible answer includes, "Choose one with a higher SPF rating."
2. Possible answer includes, "Sunscreen because it can cover all of your skin."

Life Cycles of Animals

A Dinosaur Fossil Forms

A dinosaur dies.

↓

Soft parts rot.

↓

Bones are covered with mud.

↓

Sediments cover the bones.

↓

Bones turn into rock.

↓

Layers of earth wear away.

↓

A dinosaur fossil is found!

Parts of the Rainforest

emergent layer

canopy

understory

forest floor

51409—180 Days of Science

Notes

Student Name: _____ **Date:** _____

Developing Questions Rubric

Directions: Complete this rubric every four weeks to evaluate students' Day 3 activity sheets. Only one rubric is needed per student. Their work over the four weeks can be evaluated together. Evaluate their work in each category by writing a score in each row. Then, add up their scores, and write the total on the line. Students may earn up to 5 points in each row and up to 15 points total.

Skill	5	3	1	Score
Forming Scientific Inquiries	Forms scientific inquiries related to text all or nearly all the time.	Forms scientific inquiries related to text most of the time.	Does not form scientific inquiries related to text.	
Interpreting Text	Correctly interprets texts to answer questions all or nearly all the time.	Correctly interprets texts to answer questions most of the time.	Does not correctly interpret texts to answer questions.	
Applying Information	Applies new information to form scientific questions all or nearly all the time.	Applies new information to form scientific questions most of the time.	Does not apply new information to form scientific questions.	

Total Points: _____

Student Name: _____ **Date:** _____

Planning Solutions Rubric

Directions: Complete this rubric every four weeks to evaluate students' Day 4 activity sheets. Only one rubric is needed per student. Their work over the four weeks can be evaluated together. Evaluate their work in each category by writing a score in each row. Then, add up their scores, and write the total on the line. Students may earn up to 5 points in each row and up to 15 points total.

Skill	5	3	1	Score
Planning Investigations	Plans reasonable investigations to study topics all or nearly all the time.	Plans reasonable investigations to study topics most of the time.	Does not plan reasonable investigations to study topics.	
Making Predictions	Studies events to make reasonable predictions all or nearly all the time.	Studies events to make reasonable predictions most of the time.	Does not study events to make reasonable predictions.	
Choosing Next Steps	Chooses reasonable next steps for investigations all or nearly all the time.	Chooses reasonable next steps for investigations most of the time.	Does not choose reasonable next steps for investigations.	

Total Points: _____

Student Name: _____ **Date:** _____

Communicating Results Rubric

Directions: Complete this rubric every four weeks to evaluate students' Day 5 activity sheets. Only one rubric is needed per student. Their work over the four weeks can be evaluated together. Evaluate their work in each category by writing a score in each row. Then, add up their scores, and write the total on the line. Students may earn up to 5 points in each row and up to 15 points total.

Skill	5	3	1	Score
Representing Data	Correctly represents data with charts and graphs all or nearly all the time.	Correctly represents data with charts and graphs most of the time.	Does not correctly represents data with charts and graphs.	
Making Connections	Makes reasonable connections between new information and prior knowledge all or nearly all the time.	Makes reasonable connections between new information and prior knowledge most of the time.	Does not make reasonable connections between new information and prior knowledge.	
Explaining Results	Uses evidence to accurately explain results all or nearly all the time.	Uses evidence to accurately explain results most of the time.	Does not use evidence to accurately explain results.	

Total Points: _____

Life Science Analysis Chart

Directions: Record the total of each student's Day 1 and Day 2 scores from the four weeks. Then, record each student's rubric scores (pages 210–212). Add the totals, and record the sums in the Total Scores column. Record the average class score in the last row.

Student Name	Week 4 Day 1	Day 2	DQ	PS	CR	Week 8 Day 1	Day 2	DQ	PS	CR	Week 12 Day 1	Day 2	DQ	PS	CR	Total Scores
Average Classroom Score																

DQ = Developing Questions, PS = Planning Solutions, CR = Communicating Results

Physical Science Analysis Chart

Directions: Record the total of each student's Day 1 and Day 2 scores from the four weeks. Then, record each student's rubric scores (pages 210–212). Add the totals, and record the sums in the Total Scores column. Record the average class score in the last row.

Student Name	Week 4 Day 1	Week 4 Day 2	Week 4 DQ	Week 4 PS	Week 4 CR	Week 8 Day 1	Week 8 Day 2	Week 8 DQ	Week 8 PS	Week 8 CR	Week 12 Day 1	Week 12 Day 2	Week 12 DQ	Week 12 PS	Week 12 CR	Total Scores
Average Classroom Score																

DQ = Developing Questions, PS = Planning Solutions, CR = Communicating Results

Earth and Space Science Analysis Chart

Directions: Record the total of each student's Day 1 and Day 2 scores from the four weeks. Then, record each student's rubric scores (pages 210–212). Add the totals, and record the sums in the Total Scores column. Record the average class score in the last row.

Student Name	Week 4 Day 1	Week 4 Day 2	Week 4 DQ	Week 4 PS	Week 4 CR	Week 8 Day 1	Week 8 Day 2	Week 8 DQ	Week 8 PS	Week 8 CR	Week 12 Day 1	Week 12 Day 2	Week 12 DQ	Week 12 PS	Week 12 CR	Total Scores
Average Classroom Score																

DQ = Developing Questions, PS = Planning Solutions, CR = Communicating Results

Digital Resources

To access digital resources, go to this website and enter the following code: 76143708
www.teachercreatedmaterials.com/administrators/download-files/

Rubrics

Resource	Filename
Developing Questions Rubric	questionsrubric.pdf
Planning Solutions Rubric	solutionsrubric.pdf
Communicating Results Rubric	resultsrubric.pdf

Item Analysis Sheets

Resource	Filename
Life Science Analysis Chart	LSanalysischart.pdf
	LSanalysischart.docx
	LSanalysischart.xlsx
Physical Science Analysis Chart	PSanalysischart.pdf
	PSanalysischart.docx
	PSanalysischart.xlsx
Earth and Space Science Analysis Chart	ESSanalysischart.pdf
	ESSanalysischart.docx
	ESSanalysischart.xlsx

Standards

Resource	Filename
Standards Charts	standards.pdf